W9-BHE-606

small steps for catholic moms

Your Daily Call to Think, Pray, and Act

Danielle Bean and Elizabeth Foss

Foreword by Lisa M. Hendey

AVE MARIA PRESS AVE Notre Dame, Indiana

Founded in 1865, Ave Maria Press is a ministry of the United States Province of Holy Cross.

www.avemariapress.com

Paperback: ISBN-10 1-59471-426-6, ISBN-13 978-1-59471-426-9

E-book: ISBN-10 1-59471-427-4, ISBN-13 978-1-59471-427-6

Cover image by Thinkstockphotos.com

Cover and text design by Katherine Robinson.

Printed and bound in the United States of America.

Library of Congress Cataloging-in-Publication Data is available.

❀

Danielle:

For Dan, my best friend,

who has been with me every

step of the way.

Elizabeth:

This one is for Sarah Anne,

who was with me for every word.

These saints prayed you home.

And for Patrick;

they are your saints, too,

morning by morning

of that terrible, wonderful year.

❀

To Ania!
God bless you
on this journey!
Danielle Bean ♡

Contents

Foreword

✿

It was completely on a whim that I registered the domain name "CatholicMom.com" so many years ago. As the mom of two young sons and married to the love of my life (then a non-Catholic), I recall feeling completely overwhelmed not only by my motherly duties, but especially by the responsibility of raising our children in the faith. My motivations for buying a "dummies" computer book and starting a small website were largely selfish: I was desperate for support, encouragement, and information about my vocation to motherhood, and specifically to Catholic motherhood.

Our desire to connect—to be in communion with one another—never ceases to amaze me. I now count many of the women I connected with back in those early days as dear friends. Many of them have gone on to become contributors to a resource that now welcomes hundreds of thousands of women from close to two hundred countries around the world into a daily dialogue about the things that matter most in our lives. Together we have watched our babies be born and our children grow; we have prayed with and for one another and we've done our very best to mentor the new moms who have come into our ever blossoming fold.

These many years later, I still wake up each day and head anxiously to my desk with a joy for the mission that has become my life's work. While the ways in which our Church reaches out to us have developed and diversified over the past several years, her message remains as timeless as always. And while Catholic parents may now have new trials and possibilities to face that are born of an ever advancing technological culture, many of the fears, questions, delights, and joys we hold in our hearts are the same ones our parents and grandparents before us grappled with and celebrated as we grew up.

As women, as wives and singles, as stay-at-home moms and nine-to-fivers, as mothers and grandmothers, and especially as Catholics and women of faith, we are on a mission: to know, love, and serve God, to share his loving care with our family and friends, and to enjoy life with him forever in heaven. Lofty goals, and ones that require a daily recommitment! This mission demands of us our very best. And to be at our best, we need all the help, support, and encouragement we can find.

That is why I am thrilled beyond measure to have partnered with my friends and colleagues at Ave Maria Press to create a series of resources that will support you in your life's mission. With this series of books as a compliment to our resources at

CatholicMom.com, we aim to educate, to inspire, and to uplift you with resources that are engaging and authentically Catholic. It's our great hope that these books will nurture your heart, mind, body, and soul—that they will go beyond the mainstream books you find about parenting and touch upon the cares that make our mothering not simply a status, but rather a vocation.

As a wife, mom, and woman constantly in search of both a deeper relationship with Jesus Christ and a way to manage all that's on my plate, I couldn't be more excited about the release of *Small Steps for Catholic Moms* by my dear friends Danielle Bean and Elizabeth Foss. This volume may look simple on the surface, but don't let that *Small Steps* title fool you. As any mom knows, baby steps—taken so tentatively at first and yet greeted with such profound exaltation by parents—lead toward a lifelong journey for our precious children. Indeed, our own vocational path has taken us from our own first steps as children, to the altar to be joined with our husbands, into the delivery room as we gave birth to our precious babies, and beyond. Our days are filled with running and busyness as we aim to serve and to give the best of ourselves to the competing demands in our lives.

Elizabeth and Danielle recognize both the frantic pace of the average Catholic Mom's life, as well as the great need for each of us to find time to nurture our spiritual selves. In the absence of God's presence, we lack the fuel so necessary to run the race that unfolds in our homes, workplaces, and communities each day. By giving us a simple formula for daily prayer, packed with insight, saintly role models, and inspiration to act upon our beliefs, the authors deliver the tools we need not only to run life's race, but to win its ultimate prize—an eternity spent in God's presence, surrounded by our loved ones.

As Paul's words in Hebrews remind us:

> Therefore, since we are surrounded by so great a cloud of witnesses, let us rid ourselves of every burden and sin that clings to us and persevere in running the race that lies before us.

I pray that as you join Danielle, Elizabeth, and me in starting or ending your days with *Small Steps for Catholic Moms*, you will feel nurtured and uplifted in your vocation and encouraged along your own spiritual journey towards heaven. May this book accompany your baby steps, your daily hikes, your sprints, and your strong finishes in your own life's race, and may you and your family be profoundly blessed as you journey life's path!

Lisa M. Hendey

INTRODUCTION

❁

Before you begin to read this book, we want to be clear about one thing: There are no rules. This book is not an obligation. If you begin to use it daily and then wind up setting it aside for a while, you will not have failed.

We hope that *Small Steps* will be a tool for moms to use as it suits them. Some will prefer to follow this program "by the book," using just one page each day. Others will enjoy browsing through the entire book for inspiration—or following the book diligently when they feel the need for discipline and casually when they don't. Still others might choose a particular virtue to work on and focus on that month's pages, regardless of what the calendar says.

Many mothers struggle with finding the balance between accomplishing daily duties and maintaining an active spiritual life. During our busiest mothering years, some of us might become frustrated with our inability to establish sophisticated prayer lives, while others of us might neglect our spiritual lives altogether. Neither of these is a healthy approach.

In this little volume, we offer daily prompts and suggestions—small steps—to encourage you and help you attain that elusive balance between an active life and a contemplative one. We share three items each day:

Think—Each day's entry features words from saints or Scripture. We hope that you will find in these small offerings what we did—wisdom that points you in the right direction and prompts you to further intimate conversation with our Lord.

Pray—We also offer daily words of prayer. These personal prayers were composed in the quiet of our own homes before we heard little feet on the stairs to greet the day and after we kissed sleepy children good-night. We've kept our readers close to our hearts while writing and done our best to bring all mothers' cares to God. We hope that these prayers will be just the beginning of your own fruitful prayer times.

Act—Finally, every day, we've given you a little something to do—a chance to bring your thoughts and prayers to action. By considering just one virtue a month, we focus on specific ideals that incline our hearts toward God. We pray that these prompts toward action will bless you, your family, and your community.

It is our hope that this little book will help you take small steps in the right direction—toward real spiritual growth and the fulfillment of your vocation through everyday work. The process of gathering and sharing these thoughts with you has certainly blessed us.

Big changes happen with small steps. So let's take a few . . . together.

JANUARY

Joy

JANUARY 1

SOLEMNITY OF MARY,
MOTHER OF GOD

Think

"And Mary said: 'My soul proclaims the greatness of
the Lord; my spirit rejoices in God my savior. For he has
looked upon his handmaid's lowliness; behold, from now
on will all ages call me blessed. The Mighty One has done
great things for me, and holy is his name."

~LUKE 1:46–49

Pray

Mary, I want strength of faith like yours. I want to
glorify God in my soul. I want to count all things joy.
Give me grace to become more and more like you.

Act

Gather with your family and share resolutions for
the New Year. How will you grow closer to God in
the next 365 days?

Think

"From silly devotions and sour-faced saints, good Lord, deliver us."

~St. Teresa of Avila

Pray

Thank you, God, for this new year—for the chance to begin again, for the opportunity to be a cheerful witness to the abundant joy of life in you!

Act

Are you on the road to becoming a sour-faced saint? Do you offer your devotions and go about your duties with a grim face and a resigned sigh? Lighten up! God's glory is shining around you and—if you let him—he will fill you with joy.

Think

"The condition of union seems to be nothing else than dying, so as to speak, entirely to all the things of the world, and living in the enjoyment of God."

~St. Teresa of Avila

Pray

I want to enjoy you, God. Draw my heart and mind ever closer to you so that I might find all joy and all happiness in you.

Act

It's still Christmas! Invite some friends for tea or coffee. Don't fuss about fancy table settings or decorations. Just rejoice together in the Good News of Christ's birth.

Think

"It is requisite for the relaxation of the mind that we make use, from time to time, of playful deeds and jokes."

~ST. THOMAS AQUINAS

Pray

God, help me to always hear your glad voice in the laughter of the ones I love.

Act

Pop some popcorn this afternoon and share jokes as a family. If you don't know any good ones, borrow some children's joke and riddle books from the library. Laugh together!

January 5

Think

"Let us be truly sons of Divine Providence and trust wholly in God. We are not among those doom-sayers who think that the world will end tomorrow. Corruption and evil are indeed rampant, but I still maintain that God will triumph in the end."

~St. Aloysius Orione

Pray

When all seems to be falling apart around me, Lord, help me to see things as you do. I do trust in you. Bolster my faltering faith.

Act

Plan a simple activity with your kids today. Make cocoa, make a snowman, or make a craft. As you work and play together, pay attention to the pure enjoyment your children find in small pleasures. Aim to do likewise.

Think

"Joy is a net of love by which you can catch souls. A joyful heart is the inevitable result of a heart burning with love."

~Bl. Teresa of Calcutta

Pray

Baby Jesus, how the hearts of the Magi must have swelled with the joy of seeing you! Be ever present to me and help me to bring your joy to those at home here and to those who live a great distance from me.

Act

Use gold or silver paper to wrap a small gift (perhaps a book) for each member of your family. Enjoy the Feast of the Epiphany!

JANUARY 7

Think

"Prayer reveals to souls the vanity of earthly goods and pleasures. It fills them with light, strength, and consolation; and gives them a foretaste of the calm bliss of our heavenly home."

~St. Rose of Viterbo

Pray

God, sometimes I am tempted to think I will never have peace or calm in my home or my heart. When life gets noisy and wild, remind me of the peaceful bliss that awaits us all in heaven.

Act

Sing! Even if you lack vocal talents, gather your family, put on some beautiful music, and make a joyful noise unto the Lord.

Think

"Joy is very infectious; therefore, be always full of joy."

~BL. TERESA OF CALCUTTA

Pray

God of joy, make me mindful that I set the tone in my home. Let me ring in the New Year with infectious joy!

Act

Sometimes it's sad to welcome the beginning of a new year by packing up the festive decorations of Christmas. Light a new candle for January and remember to keep singing even after the caroling season is over. Your light and song will be infectious.

Think

"If we wish to serve God and love our neighbor well, we must manifest our joy in the service we render to him and them. Let us open wide our hearts. It is Joy which invites us. Press forward and fear nothing."

~St. Katherine Drexel

Pray

Dear God, show me the joy that there is to be found in embracing your will today—one moment at a time, one thought at a time, one act at a time.

Act

Do you remember a time when you met someone so joyful you could not help but feel uplifted by his or her presence? Remember what an attractive force that kind of joy is and aim to be a joyful, attractive force to someone else today.

Think

"It is above all in the home that, before ever a word is spoken, children should experience God's love in the love which surrounds them."

~BL. JOHN PAUL II

Pray

Dear sweet Lord, before I open my mouth to speak, help me to relax my shoulders and smile. Then, let whatever comes out of my mouth be an expression of your love.

Act

How do your children experience God's love in your home? When we smile, our faces reflect the joy we have in knowing we are loved unconditionally by our benevolent Father. Smile at your family today—often.

Think

"O Death, where is your sting? O Hades, where is your victory? Christ is risen and life is freed, Christ is risen and the tomb is emptied of the dead: for Christ, being risen from the dead, has become the Leader and Reviver of those who had fallen asleep. To Him be glory and power for ever and ever."

~St. John Chrysostom

Pray

I know the Good News, Lord, but help me to *really* know it. I want to feel it in my bones and exude it from every pore of my body. Fill my heart and soul with such overflowing joy that it reveals itself to everyone I meet.

Act

Visit a nursing home with your kids (or someone else's) today. Sing songs to the residents, read to them, ask them questions about their past, or tell them jokes or funny stories. Bring them all the joy you have inside and do your best to leave them smiling.

JANUARY 12

Think

"They are led and bound more by gentleness than by force or harsh words."

~St. Catherine of Siena

Pray

God, grant me the strength and grace to be gentle and joyful in all I say and do today.

Act

A mother's gentleness springs from the joy of knowing that God is kind and merciful. Just for today, do not speak a word of harshness or frustration; enjoy your family instead. If you blow it, humble yourself and apologize right away.

Think

"It is better for us to reach eternal bliss after a few difficulties than to go down into the depths of hell after brief joy."
~St. Caesarius of Arles

Pray

God, it's sometimes awfully easy to focus on here and now, at the expense of my spiritual growth. Give me a taste of the joys that await me in heaven and help me remember that my real happiness will not be found in this world.

Act

Write a list of all the things that bring you joy. Then write a second list of all the ways you can bring joy to others—especially your family. Fill your day with as many of the things on the first list as you can. Do as many things on the second list as you can.

January 14

Think

"When many men rejoice together, there is a richer joy in each individual, since they enkindle themselves and they inflame one another."

~St. Augustine

Pray

God, you created me for community. Help me to grow in hospitality. Give me grace to open my heart and home with joy.

Act

Invite friends to eat a simple soup and bread supper with you tonight. Build a fire in the fireplace. Enjoy the company of good companions.

January 15

Think

"Contemplation is nothing else than a secret, peaceful, and loving infusion of God, which if admitted, will set the soul on fire with the Spirit of love."

~St. John of the Cross

Pray

God, give me the grace to count my blessings instead of my crosses, my gains instead of my losses. Make me a joyful servant in all that I think and do and say today.

Act

Plan a family movie night tonight. Watch *It's a Wonderful Life* or some other family favorite. Snuggle with your husband and kids and revel in God's goodness.

Think

"In the family, women have the opportunity to transmit the faith in the early training of their children. They are particularly responsible for the joyful task of leading them to discover the supernatural world."

~Bl. John Paul II

Pray

God, I find you and your supernatural world in your Word. Remind me to share the joy of scripture with my children every day.

Act

Read a Bible story to a young child today.

JANUARY 17

Think

"As the result of sin, the virtues have become painful to us; we shrink from them because they mean humiliation and suffering. You do not want to be humiliated? Humiliation is an honor, suffering a joy, because Jesus Christ has placed in them true honor and true joy."

~St. Peter Julian Eymard

Pray

God, our fallen world and our fallen human nature fail to see you as a source of real joy. We avoid sacrifice and suffering that can bring us closer to you. Help me to see and understand the paradox of the Cross.

Act

Choose something small that causes you to suffer. Starting right now, offer it joyfully to God today.

Think

"I sometimes reflect on the great damage parents do by not striving that their children might always see virtuous deeds of every kind."

~St. Teresa of Avila

Pray

God, please don't let me miss the opportunities you give me every day to practice virtue in front of my children. Grant them the grace of virtuous examples of every kind.

Act

The expression of joy in Christian life is a virtue. Too often, though, mothers feel the weight of the world on their shoulders. And it shows! Today, walk and talk and smile as if you have the joy of Jesus in your heart and soul.

Think

"Prayer is a wine that makes glad the heart of men."

~St. Bernard of Clairvaux

Pray

I seek happiness in many things, God: human relationships, food, work, sex, and money. I am sorry for the times I have put these things above you. I want to give you the first place in my heart always.

Act

Add more family prayer time to your day today. Even if you usually pray together at bedtime, add something more—an afternoon Rosary or the Angelus. Rejoice together in God's presence.

Think

"The very sight of God causes delight. Hence he who sees God cannot be without delight."

~St. Thomas Aquinas

Pray

Thank you, God, for delighting my soul with the many gifts with which you grace my life!

Act

Where do you see God? Is he in the winter world outside your door? In the adoration chapel? In the eyes of the child pleading for another story and a cup of hot chocolate? Seize the delight he has waiting there for you today!

Think

"I know well that joy is not in the things that surround us; it dwells in the innermost soul."

~St. Thérèse of Lisieux

Pray

God, as I go about my work today, keep me looking inward—toward you and the depths of happiness that can only be found in you.

Act

Set an alarm for 9:00 a.m., 12:00 p.m., 3:00 p.m., and 6:00 p.m. today. Every time it rings, offer your circumstances—whatever they may be—to God. Give him your heart and return to your duties with joy.

Think

"A glad spirit attains to perfection more quickly than any other."

~St. Philip Neri

Pray

God, make me ever mindful of my true desire: to be perfect as my Father in heaven is perfect.

Act

Are you plagued by perfectionism? Do you get mired in the heavy details as you quest after the impossible human standard of perfection? Let it go! Today, quest after a glad spirit and let God show you his plan for perfection.

Think

"The compass remains always in its place, turning towards the pole. Here is the point: we must be careful to keep the compass of our will in order, that it may never turn elsewhere than to the pole of the divine pleasure."

~St. Francis de Sales

Pray

God, even though I find pleasure in many licit, earthly things, help me to recall that you alone are the kind of pleasure that lasts forever.

Act

Spend some time outdoors today—go for a walk or just sit quietly and observe nature. Give thanks to God that all of his creatures are so fearfully and wonderfully made.

Think

"We all in fact need an occasional period of extended physical, psychological, and spiritual rest. Especially for those who live in large cities, it is important that they immerse themselves in nature for a while. For a vacation to be truly such and bring genuine well-being, in it a person must recover a good balance within himself, with others, and with the environment. It is this interior and exterior harmony which revitalizes the mind and reinvigorates the body and spirit."

~BL. JOHN PAUL II

Pray

Sometimes, God, I'm overcome by the inertia of my ordinary work days. Help me to shake myself awake and allow myself time and space for rest and relaxation.

Act

Have you been stuck inside, working incessantly this winter? It's time to stretch and move outdoors. Even if a vacation is not possible for you right now, take a day or a half day to change your routine and enjoy some recreation. Allow God to revitalize and reinvigorate you.

Think

"*Perform faithfully what God requires of you each moment, and leave the thought of everything else to him. I assure you that to live in this way will give you great peace.*"

~St. Jane Frances de Chantal

Pray

I long to give you everything, O God, and yet I am weak and fickle like a child. Hold me, and remind me, moment by moment, that you are with me and that I can do all things through you.

Act

Hug every person in your household today—even the big kids who might resist it. In fact, *especially* the big kids who might resist it.

Think

"Be merry, really merry. The life of a true Christian should be a perpetual jubilee, a prelude to the festivals of eternity."

~ST. THEOPHANE VENARD

Pray

Don't let me look down, Lord, when I carry the cross you've chosen for me. Let me look up and whistle while I work!

Act

How do you make merry in your home? Do you bake a cake? Play a game of backyard soccer? Have an impromptu family concert or sing-along? Do it!

Think

"To keep the soul continually in a state of gentle calm, it is necessary to perform every action as being done in the presence of God, and as if he himself had ordained it."

~St. Francis de Sales

Pray

God, sometimes it's so hard to let go of control! Help me to trust that you are in charge and to find the peace and joy that comes from accepting each moment for the gift it truly is.

Act

What makes your family laugh? Looking at old photo albums, retelling funny stories, telling jokes, or watching a comedy? Whatever it is, make time for that today.

Think

"When spiritual joy fills hearts, the Serpent throws off his deadly poison in vain. The devils cannot harm the servant of Christ when they see he is filled with holy joy."

~St. Francis of Assisi

Pray

God, I am so grateful that nothing—not even the devil—is bigger than you are. Fill me with your joy and protect us from the evil one. Enable me to be open to your perfect grace.

Act

Make little tarts today. Press cookie dough into muffin tins to make cups. Bake. Fill them with sweet custard or pudding. Remind your children (and yourself!) that God always fills us with sweetness and joy, if only we let him.

Think

"One cuts herself out a cross of pride; another, one of causeless discontent; another, one of restless impatience or peevish fretfulness. Yet we know certainly that our God calls us to a holy life, that he gives us every grace, every abundant grace; and though we are weak of ourselves, this grace is able to carry us through every obstacle and difficulty."

~St. Elizabeth Ann Seton

Pray

Take all my sorrows, worries, pains, and complaints today, God. Release me from them; ensure that I will not burden anyone else with these trifles today.

Act

Play make-believe with a child today. Sail the ocean, be a lion, take a trip to Mars. Anything is possible. Rejoice in that!

Think

"Whatever did not fit in with my plan did lie within the plan of God. I have an ever deeper and firmer belief that nothing is merely an accident when seen in the light of God, that my whole life down to the smallest details has been marked out for me in the plan of Divine Providence and has a completely coherent meaning in God's all-seeing eyes. And so I am beginning to rejoice in the light of glory wherein this meaning will be unveiled to me."

~ST. EDITH STEIN

Pray

I see the light of your glory in my life, Lord. Let me trust you with my plans and let me rejoice always in your goodness and mercy!

Act

Make a list of all the times your plan did not lie within the plan of God. Now, list the lessons you learned and the ways he shaped your soul during those times. Be truly thankful for the times our plans went awry. Rejoice in God's wisdom and grace!

JANUARY 31

Think

"Seek union with God and buoy yourself up with hope—that sure virtue!—because Jesus will illuminate the way for you with the light of his mercy, even in the darkest night."

~St. Josemaria Escriva

Pray

When I am fumbling in the dark, Lord, bring me your light. Show me your mercy, and fill my heart with irrepressible goodness and joy.

Act

Think of someone who has recently suffered a loss of some kind. Invite that person to your home and share God's joy with him or her. Be Christ to that person, and help him or her to heal.

Simplicity

FEBRUARY 1

Think

"The more man uses moderation in his life, the more he is at peace, for he is not full of cares for many things."

~St. Anthony the Great

Pray

My life is full of many things, God. Help me to see all things as tools and not goals.

Act

Where do books and papers pile up in your house? Spend fifteen minutes taming the pile today. File, return, and throw away.

FEBRUARY 2

Think

"God hasn't called me to be successful. He called me to be faithful."

~BL. TERESA OF CALCUTTA

Pray

Jesus, help me to remember that it doesn't matter how many things I cross off my to-do list if I am not kind and charitable and gentle as I do them.

Act

Instead of focusing on the outcomes of your activities today, focus simply on your state of soul as you do them. As you work, don't sin.

Think

"He is rich enough who is poor with Christ."

~St. Jerome

Pray

Thank you, God, for all the ways you provide for me and my family. Give your help to those who are not as blessed as we are.

Act

See how long you can go without spending any money. A day? A few days? A week? Longer? Give thanks to God for the abundance you enjoy.

Think

"You know that our Lord does not look at the greatness or difficulty of our action, but at the love with which you do it. What, then, have you to fear?"

~St. Thérèse of Lisieux

Pray

I know that it is not a complex thing to express my love in little ways, Jesus. Illuminate those little ways for me so that I don't miss the opportunities.

Act

Think of one small thing which will surprise the people you love today. A note in a lunchbox? A chore done by you before they could do it? An unexpected backrub? Do it.

Think

"Be not anxious about what you have, but about what you are."

~Pope St. Gregory the Great

Pray

"You can't take it with you" is a cliché, but it's an important one to remember. Show me where I am too attached to earthly things, God, so that I might detach myself from them.

Act

Go through your bedroom closet today. Give any clothing items you haven't worn in the last two years to a friend or to a charity.

Think

"Take care not to meddle in things which do not concern you, nor even allow them to pass through your mind; for perhaps you will not then be able to fulfill your own task."

~St. John of the Cross

Pray

God, help me to keep my eyes—and my mind—on my own work.

Act

Look at your reading, computer, and television habits. Eliminate those things which don't truly concern you.

Think

"We should be simple in our affections, intentions, actions, and words; we should do what we find to do without artifice or guile."

~St. Vincent de Paul

Pray

I want to follow you today, Lord. Show me where you want me to go.

Act

When you see something that needs doing today (laundry to put away, a bed to be made, a table to be cleared, etc.), don't procrastinate and make excuses. See God's will for your day in the sight of those tasks, and just do them.

FEBRUARY 8

Think

"True simplicity is like that of children, who think, speak, and act candidly and without craftiness. . . . They have no care or thought for themselves."

~St. Francis de Sales

Pray

How many times do I make things more complicated by my complex words and actions! Please forgive me for the times I've taken your peaceful, serene world and muddied it up with my own orchestrations. Please God, unite my will to yours and let me act in simplicity with the knowledge that I'm doing what you would have me do, and only that.

Act

Choose one issue that has been troubling you lately. Take it to prayer and ensure you understand what your heavenly Father wants you to do. Go to the parties concerned and speak directly and candidly about it—no craftiness.

Think

"A detached man should always be looking to see what he can do without."

~BL. HENRY SUSO

Pray

I want to focus more on you, God. Help me to see what activities I should cut back on to make more room for you.

Act

Pray a decade of the Rosary today. If you are too busy to pray a decade of the Rosary, you are too busy.

Think

"The way to love anything is to realize that it may be lost."
~G. K. CHESTERTON

Pray

Never let me forget, Lord, that life itself is a precious gift. Let all my days on earth be spent knowing that my true treasure is in heaven.

Act

If you lost your life and had to make an accounting of how you'd spent it, what would that look like? Go about your day today treating people as if this was your last day on earth. Do the important things.

Think

"I am a little pencil in the hand of a writing God who is sending a love letter to the world."

~Bl. Teresa of Calcutta

Pray

Let me be your instrument, O Lord. Use my voice, my hands, and my gifts to bring your love to others.

Act

Make a gift for someone you love today, using your own hands. Draw, sew, bake, or write by hand and deliver the gift in person.

Think

"There is a kind of simplicity that causes a person to close his eyes to all sentiments of nature and to human considerations, and fix them interiorly upon the holy maxims of the Faith that he may guide himself in every work by their means, in such a way that in all his actions, words, thoughts, interests and vicissitudes, at all times and in all places, he may always recur to and do nothing except by them and according to them. This is an admirable simplicity."

~St. Vincent de Paul

Pray

Jesus, let me draw strength from your journey to Calvary. Help me to shoulder my crosses and give little notice to their heaviness, their roughness, or their unwieldiness.

Act

Do you have a trigger? Someone or something that always causes you to grit your teeth and clench your jaw? Today, when faced with that trigger, think instead of Jesus on the cross. Forgive, embrace, be kind. Smile.

FEBRUARY 13

Think

"Don't forget it: he has much who needs least. Don't create necessities for yourself."

~ST. JOSEMARIA ESCRIVA

Pray

Give me a simple heart, Lord. I want only to love.

Act

Give your children the gift of open space. Go through their toy boxes today. Give away, throw away, and put away as many items as possible.

FEBRUARY 14

Think

"I just take one day. Yesterday is gone. Tomorrow has not come. We have only today to love Jesus."

~BL. TERESA OF CALCUTTA

Pray

Jesus, show me whom you want me to love today. Give me the grace to love well.

Act

Valentine's Day can be a very lonely day for some people. Find someone unloved, someone who might even seem unlovable, and bless him or her this day. Do something small and thoughtful: a phone call, a favor, a sweet treat, a bunch of flowers. Do it with all your heart for Jesus.

FEBRUARY 15

Think

"We can afford to lose castles, but we cannot let a day go by without attending Holy Mass."

~BL. CHARLES OF BLOIS

Pray

I can be so distracted at Mass! Help me rein in my thoughts and focus on your presence in the Eucharist.

Act

Go to Mass today. Focus on the gift of Christ in the Eucharist and nothing else.

FEBRUARY 16

Think

"Become more and more a soul who is simple and confident in our good Savior. Confide everything to Him; bring everything to Him, and He will give you all that is necessary."

~ST. FRANCES DE SALES AVIAT

Pray

Remind me, Lord, whenever I am tempted to acquire more "stuff," that nothing I can buy will truly satisfy my heart.

Act

We tend to gather things that we think will make us happy, but often it's those things that crowd peace out of our lives. Conquer some clutter today. Begin in just one room and eliminate anything there that doesn't truly bring you peace of heart. Simplicity in your environment will support simplicity in your soul.

Think

"I think the greatest happiness of this life is to be released from the cares and formalities of what is called the world. My world is my family, and all the change to me will be that I can devote myself unmolested to my treasure."

~ST. ELIZABETH ANN SETON

Pray

Lord, when I begin to worry about money, give me a nudge. Remind me of your generous love and your unfailing providence.

Act

Take a look at your monthly or weekly budget. Find something "extra" you could do without and give it up—for one week or one month. Consider giving it up for good.

February 18

Think

"Simplicity is nothing but an act of charity, pure and simple, which has but one sole end—that of gaining the love of God. Our soul is then truly simple, when we have no aim at all but this, in all we do."

~St. Francis de Sales

Pray

Jesus, you lived out perfect simplicity by living out perfect charity. I've taken on a challenge today which will require supernatural grace. Infuse my whole being with your love, so that I might respond to everyone as you would today.

Act

We sometimes confuse "easy" with "simple." St. Francis challenges us to true simplicity—and that's not easy. Be purposeful today. Let everything you do, big or small, be done with pure charity. It won't be easy, but it will be simple.

Think

"What do superfluous riches profit in this world when they do not assist our birth or impede our dying? We are born into this world naked, we leave without a cent, we are buried without our inheritance."

~St. Ambrose

Pray

Lord, show me the biggest way that I tend to waste time. Give me grace to take greater control of that part of my life today.

Act

If there is some activity you think wastes your time (TV, computer, telephone, etc.), give it up today. See what opportunities arise in the pockets of time you free up.

FEBRUARY 20

Think

"We must pray without tiring, for the salvation of mankind does not depend on material success; nor on sciences that cloud the intellect. Neither does it depend on arms and human industries, but on Jesus alone."

~St. Frances Xavier Cabrini

Pray

God, help me to keep my prayer commitments. Never tire of reminding me to begin and end my day with you. Thank you for being ready and willing and happy to be with me whenever I slow myself to simply sit in your presence.

Act

Prayer is so simple, but we never get to it as much as we should. Carve out an extra fifteen minutes today to sit alone, light a candle, and just be with Jesus. Read a short gospel verse, ask him to speak to you, and sit quietly and listen. Just before you blow out the candle, pray for the intentions of your friends.

Think

"You, who have the kingdom of heaven, are not a poor little woman, but a queen."

~BL. HENRY SUSO

Pray

Keep me focused on heavenly goals today, Lord. Truly, nothing else matters.

Act

Is there some soul you continually forget to pray for? Perhaps a deceased relative or friend? Take time today to light a candle and pray for that person's eternal salvation.

Think

"Poverty was not found in heaven. It abounded on earth, but man does not know its value. The Son of God, therefore, treasured it and came down from heaven to choose it for Himself, to make it precious to us."

~St. Bernard of Clairvaux

Pray

Strip me of all my "extras" Lord. Show me who I really am, and how I might grow in love and simplicity.

Act

How much money do you put in the collection basket at church on Sunday? This week, set aside just a bit more. Set it aside and forget about it. It's God's money, not yours.

Think

"Jesus needs neither books nor Doctors of Divinity in order to instruct souls; He, the Doctor of Doctors, He teaches without noise of words."

~St. Thérèse of Lisieux

Pray

I talk too much, Lord. Keep me quiet today. Make me still. Teach me.

Act

Find a way to show each of your family members that you love them today—without saying a word.

Think

"Kind words can be short and easy to speak, but their echoes are truly endless."

~BL. TERESA OF CALCUTTA

Pray

Bl. Teresa, please pray that nothing but sweet kindness will escape my lips today.

Act

We are surrounded by examples of witty repartee and sly sarcasm. Our culture is hungry for sweet words of kindness. In all your conversations today, from the most casual to the most intimate, endeavor to speak kindly. Watch for the echoes of that kindness. Particularly in your home, kindness lightens the atmosphere and sweetens relationships.

February 25

Think

"There is one only thing to do here below: to love Jesus, to win souls for him so that he may be loved. Let us seize with jealous care every least opportunity of self-sacrifice. Let us refuse him nothing—he does so want our love!"

~St. Thérèse of Lisieux

Pray

I do love you, Jesus. Clear my mind and give me a singular sense of purpose. Prepare me to love you better.

Act

How humbly and simply would you serve your family if Jesus was in your living room watching? Serve them that way today. Because he is.

Think

"When a simple soul is to act, it considers only what it is suitable to do or say and then immediately begins the action, without losing time in thinking what others will do or say about it. . . . It has no other aim than to please God."

~ST. FRANCIS DE SALES

Pray

St. Francis, please intercede for me. Beg for me the grace to know what is suitable to do or say. Ask that I might have the fortitude and discipline to do and say only that, forsaking all others for God alone.

Act

One of the greatest obstacles to simplicity in a woman's life is the cacophony of worldly voices that offer opinions and demands. Silence them today. Do that immediately, and then do the next thing God asks. Be single-minded and purposeful.

Think

"A bird can be held by a chain or a thread, still it cannot fly."

~St. John of the Cross

Pray

Is there something small in my life that is standing between me and greater love for you today, God? Show it to me. I want to rip it out.

Act

Do not sigh today. Do not roll your eyes. Do not say "in a minute." Be simply present in every moment and simply resigned to God's will.

FEBRUARY 28

Think

"Behold, I am sending you like sheep in the midst of wolves; so be shrewd as serpents and simple as doves."

~MATTHEW 10:16

Pray

Creator God, whom have you made me to be? Help me to see myself as clearly as you see me. Help me to be shrewd and nurture me as I grow into the woman you created me to be. You are the Good Shepherd—protect me and guide me on your path.

Act

Take a few minutes today to remember the dreams of the little girl you once were. Perhaps these aspirations are seeds planted by the Holy Spirit. How simple were your little girl dreams? Claim them and ask for the grace to discern whether they are truly his will for the adult life you can choose to live.

MARCH

Sacrifice

March 1

Think

"Be it little or much, be content with what you have, and pay no heed to him who would disparage your home."

~Sirach 29:23

Pray

Dear God, it's hard for me to let go of things I think I have a "right" to—like a good night's sleep or time to myself. Help me to find contentment in accepting these small sacrifices whenever you allow me the opportunity.

Act

What are you attached to? Something sweet? A cup of coffee? Television? Time online? Indulge just a little less today and give the "extra" to God.

MARCH 2

Think

"Unhappy is the soul enslaved by anything that is mortal."

~St. Augustine

Pray

If I am honest, Lord, the things that weigh on me are mortal things. When I walk in faith and remember that you have a plan for me, I am at peace. Remind me that you want me to walk with my hand firmly in your friendship. Don't let me enslave myself to mortal things.

Act

Resolve to spend fifteen minutes a day this month in silent prayer. Let God show you where you are enslaved and ask him to set you free. Put those fifteen minutes on your schedule and honor God with them every single day this month. Keep track of your progress in a journal.

Think

"The Lord is my shepherd; there is nothing I lack."

~PSALM 23:1

Pray

You truly are my shepherd Lord. Why then am I so fearful of losing "my things" sometimes? Why do I fret about making sure there is enough time and enough money for everything I want? You are all I want, and you are always right here, waiting for me. Help me remember that.

Act

Write out the Psalm from above and post it on your refrigerator, car dashboard, computer monitor, or bathroom mirror. Every time you see it, stop and pray it.

MARCH 4

Think

"There is nothing more wicked than to love money."

~St. Anthony of Padua

Pray

I love you, Lord! Help me to detach from any affection for money. I want to live my life in service to you, not in bondage to money.

Act

Look carefully at your grocery budget and your grocery list. For this week, swap out some of the more expensive items for less expensive ones. For example, trade a meat meal for a bean meal. Write a check to charity for the amount of the money you save.

MARCH 5

Think

"Let us learn from Jesus in the manger, to hold the things of the world in such esteem as they deserve."

~ST. FRANCIS DE SALES

Pray

No excuses today, Lord! I am all done telling you about what I can't afford to give or do. Today, I want to give and give as you do—with wild, reckless abandon. Give me grace to do that.

Act

How much money were you planning to give to your church this week? Increase it by at least half, but don't put it on your credit card. Make up the difference by skipping something else in your budget this week—even something you might consider "essential." Ask yourself: What would Baby Jesus in the manger consider "essential?"

Think

"Your life consists of drawing nearer to God. To do this, you must detach from visible things and remember that in a short time they will be taken from you."

~BL. JOHN OF AVILA

Pray

St. Anne, patroness of homemakers, help me to inspire a detachment project in our home this spring. Pray that we can let go of anything that keeps us from drawing nearer to God. Please stay with me through this task! Keep praying that I will be a faithful steward in my home, clearing the clutter and creating a truly holy, simple, and domestic church.

Act

Begin to de-clutter. Label three boxes: give away, throw away, and put away. Enlist the help of your family and work your way through your home with those boxes.

Think

"Do not store up for yourselves treasures on earth, where moth and decay destroy, and thieves break in and steal. But store up treasures in heaven, where neither moth nor decay destroys, nor thieves break in and steal. For where your treasure is, there also will your heart be."

~MATTHEW 6:19–21

Pray

I have too many treasures, Lord. I treasure money, time, food, sleep, entertainment, attention, and the admiration of others. Show me one treasure today that displeases you, that I might rid myself of attachment to it forever.

Act

Skip all forms of sugar today. Ask God to use this small sacrifice to make you "sweeter" to your family.

March 8

Think

"When we hear people talk of riches, honors, and amusements of the world, let us remember that all things have an end, and let us then say: 'My God, I wish for thee alone and nothing more.'"

~St. Alphonsus Liguori

Pray

St. Alphonsus Liguori, I live in a culture where most people assume they have a right to be entertained and amused at the flip of a switch. Help me to pause before sitting idly in front of a screen and to choose instead to do something which will make me and my family truly happy.

Act

Give up screen time today.

Think

"What profit is there for one to gain the whole world and forfeit his life?"

~MARK 8:36

Pray

Dear God, I like to pretend I am detached from worldly things, and I can talk a pretty good game . . . until someone comes to take away my washing machine, my computer, or my car, that is. Help me to see what kinds of sacrifices I am loathe to make and give me strength to make progress in those areas.

Act

If you can help it, don't drive anywhere today or use the telephone or computer. Move your mind away from thinking of these modern luxuries as "essential" and toward a spirit of gratitude for all of God's blessings.

MARCH 10

Think

"In detachment, the spirit finds quiet and repose for coveting nothing. Nothing wearies it by elation, and nothing oppresses it by dejection, because it stands in the center of its own humility."

~St. John of the Cross

Pray

There is so much noise around me, Lord! Sometimes, I can hardly hear myself think. And I can't hear you. Help me to see the things from which I need to detach in order to achieve the peace I so dearly want.

Act

What adds noise to your life? Is it the television? Is it incessant, mindless clicking at the computer? Is it listening to the opinions of too many other people? Being riveted to bad news? Claim some quiet. Turn away from the screen and all its noise.

MARCH 11

Think

"There is an appointed time for everything, and a time for every affair under the heavens."

Pray

God, sometimes I resent what the Church requires of me. Everyone else seems to have such a fun and easy life while mine feels burdened by rules and sacrifice. Help me to see that suffering brings me closer to you and that the time for feasting is yet to come.

Act

Fast from complaining today. Make sure every thought you give voice to is a positive and helpful thought. Even when you are tired and frustrated, find a way to compliment instead of complain.

Think

"*Nothing is anything more to me; everything is nothing to me, but Jesus: neither things nor persons, neither ideas nor emotions, neither honor nor sufferings. Jesus is for me honor, delight, heart, and soul.*"

~St. Bernadette Soubirous

Pray

God, help me to see that my good ideas are your gifts and my bad ideas mean I'm not listening to you carefully enough.

Act

Be sure to notice someone else's good ideas today. Praise him or her sincerely.

Think

"Then he said to the crowd, 'Take care to guard against all greed, for though one may be rich, one's life does not consist of possessions.'"

~LUKE 12:15

Pray

God, I want to give more to you. Give me the grace I need to be more generous with my time, my talent, and my money.

Act

Look over your plan for Lent this year. How is it going? Change what needs changing and redouble your efforts as needed.

Think

"Let us detach ourselves in spirit from all that we see and cling to that which we believe. This is the cross which we must imprint on all our daily actions and behavior."

~St. Peter Damian

Pray

Open my eyes, sweet Jesus. Let me see those things to which I am clinging so that I can unclench my fist. Help me open my hand and place it firmly in yours.

Act

To fast today, do not eat anything except that which your family members have left on their plates at the end of meals. All those crusts from children's sandwiches, the last of the meat that is a bit over-done, potatoes that touched the creamed corn and so became distasteful for your toddler: those are your sustenance. Detach from eating only that which you want.

Think

"Oh what a pity it is to see some souls, like rich ships, loaded with a precious freight of good works, spiritual exercises, virtues and favors from God, which, for want of courage to make an end of some miserable little fancy or affection, can never arrive at the port of divine union, while it only needs one good earnest effort to break asunder that thread of attachment!"

~St. John Chrysostom

Pray

I am like the rich and burdened ships, O Lord. Relieve me of the burden of my attachments. Help me to see material things for the fleeting fancies they are and to focus only on you and your eternal love.

Act

Sacrifice your time today. Sit and play a board game with your toddler, read a book to a grade-school child, or just be there for a teenager. Call an elderly relative and listen to him or her tell stories you've heard a thousand times. When your husband is home, make time to just sit and be with him, doing whatever he enjoys, without regard to your own pressing needs and schedule.

MARCH 16

Think

"Consider the shortness of time, the length of eternity, and reflect on how everything down here below comes to an end and passes by. Of what use is it to lean upon that which cannot give support?"

~St. Gerard Majella

Pray

God, grant me the grace to see this day for the gift that it is and not to waste a single moment of it.

Act

If you find yourself in a coffee shop or a fast food restaurant today, pay in advance for the person behind you. Be sure to duck out before he or she knows it was you!

MARCH 17

Think

"If I be worthy, I live for my God to teach the heathen, even though they may despise me."

~ST. PATRICK

Pray

Lord, sometimes I get so tired of repeating myself. It feels like I am always reminding my kids to do their work, to get along, and to obey. Help me to recall that I am your humble messenger and to offer my annoyances for their sanctification.

Act

Make a St. Patrick treat today—Irish soda bread, cookies, "green milk," or a special meal. Tell your family the story of St. Patrick's steadfast faith, even in the face of adversity.

Think

"He is rich in spirit who has riches in his spirit, or his spirit in riches. He is poor in spirit who has neither riches in his spirit, nor his spirit in riches."

~St. Francis de Sales

Pray

God, show me how to enrich the lives of my children today. Help me to see your desire for their spiritual nourishment.

Act

Make a healthy snack and sit and read a good spiritual book to your children today.

Think

"St. Joseph was an ordinary sort of man on whom God relied to do great things. He did exactly what the Lord wanted him to do, in each and every event that went to make up his life."

~St. Josemaria Escriva

Pray

St. Joseph, sometimes I make the mistake of thinking my life must be extraordinary in order to be holy. Help me to see that holiness lies in ordinary, everyday faithfulness to God's will.

Act

Celebrate St. Joseph's unfailing faith today. Read the parts of the Bible where he is mentioned and note how quiet and how faithful he was, even when all seemed to be falling apart.

Think

"There is a vast difference between having poison and being poisoned. Doctors have all kinds of poisons for their use, but they are not poisoned. In a like manner, you may possess riches without being poisoned by them, provided you have them for use, and not by love in your heart."

~ST. FRANCIS DE SALES

Pray

Help me today, Lord, to see those things in my life that are useless, that clutter my space and burden my soul. Then, give me the strength and courage to purge.

Act

Get two trash bags. Going from room to room in your house, fill one with items to give to the needy and fill the other with trash. Throw away the trash and put the "give away" bag in your car as soon as you are finished.

Think

"The soul ought to strip itself of all things created in order to arrive at the state of abandonment."

~FR. JEAN-PIERRE DE CAUSSADE

Pray

I want to abandon myself to you God, but I am afraid. I am afraid of pain, afraid of humiliation, afraid of failure. Unburden me of my fears so that I might draw closer to you.

Act

What's holding you back from giving more of yourself to others? Shyness? Financial insecurity? Worry about what others might think? Pick one of those fears and overcome it today. Give a bit more—of your time, your talents, your money, and yourself.

MARCH 22

Think

"Riches are not forbidden, but the pride of them is."

~ST. JOHN CHRYSOSTOM

Pray

I may not have a lot of worldly riches, but I am blessed. Today, show me someone with whom I can share from my abundance.

Act

Send a care package to a college student (perhaps someone from your church or neighborhood). Offer them encouragement as they head into the last month of their semester. Include things such as granola bars, instant flavored coffee, tea bags, a stress ball, fun pens and pencils, sunflower seeds or pistachios, popcorn, a music gift card, holy water, and a rosary.

Think

"Accustom your heart to be docile, manageable, submissive, and ready to yield to all in all lawful things, for the love of your most sweet Lord; so will you become like the dove which receives all the colors which the sun gives it."

~St. Francis de Sales

Pray

Is there some part of me that I am holding back from you, Lord? Tell me what it is that I might let go and belong more completely to you.

Act

Gather your kids and go through their toys. Fill boxes with things to give away, erring on the side of generosity. Make sure to go through some of your "toys" too—appliances, clothing, books, movies, and other "treasures." Immediately make a trip to a friend's house or a charity with your donations, before you have a chance to change your mind.

Think

"I amassed for myself silver and gold, and the wealth of kings and provinces. . . . Nothing that my eyes desired did I deny them, nor did I deprive myself of any joy, but my heart rejoiced in the fruit of all my toil. But when I turned to all the works that my hands had wrought, and to the toil at which I had taken such pains, behold! All was vanity and a chase after wind, with nothing gained under the sun."

~ECCLESIASTES 2:8–11

Pray

Sometimes, I am guilty of the sin of sensuality. I am not happy unless my house is perfectly tidy and my life perfectly orderly. Forgive me! Help me to see today that a life that is ordered toward you will not always look beautiful and please my senses.

Act

Do you have birdfeeders? If so, it's time to clean them and get them ready for the returning birds. If not, it's time to go to the bird store and make an investment in feathered friends. You'll be glad you did!

Think

"Observe that perfection is not acquired by sitting with our arms folded, but it is necessary to work in earnest, in order to conquer ourselves and to bring ourselves to live not according to our inclinations and passions, but according to reason . . . and obedience. The thing is hard, it cannot be denied, but necessary. With practice, however, it becomes easy and pleasing."

~St. Francis de Sales

Pray

Sometimes obedience feels like the greatest sacrifice, Lord! I would so much rather do things my own way; and yet I know that your will is that my own should be bent. Especially in my family life, help me to accommodate the wants and needs of others.

Act

Take time today to really listen to what your family wants and needs from you. Look people in the eyes when they speak and ask them to share what needs they are feeling today. Then do your best to meet them.

MARCH 26

Think

"Those who risk all for God will find that they have both lost all and gained all."

~St. Teresa of Avila

Pray

God, show me what you would have me risk for you!

Act

Is there something that your husband has been asking you to do? A trip? A movie? A night without the kids you are sure you can't possibly get away for? Make concrete plans to do it.

Think

"The way to do all well is to attend solely to the one we have in hand, taking care to do it as perfect as possible, and banishing for the time the thought of every other; and when this is finished, not to think of it anymore, but to think of what remains to be done."

~FR. M. D'AVILA

Pray

Dear God, it's so easy to be distracted. Keep me focused on the task at hand and protect me from worries about what my work will cost me in time, money, and pride. Give me grace today to give without counting and without expecting anything in return.

Act

Whenever you are in the car today, keep the radio turned off. God might have something to tell you, but he isn't going to shout it over the country music station.

Think

"A great aid to going against your will is to bear in mind continually how all is vanity and how quickly everything comes to an end. This helps to remove our attachment to trivia and center on what will never end."

~St. Teresa of Avila

Pray

God, show me the trivia in my life. Divert my attention from the fleeting and help me to focus on eternity.

Act

Do you have a habit that makes you a slave to the trivial? Replace it today with a virtuous habit.

Think

"What are the works upon which all our profit and all our perfection depends? All those which is our lot to perform, but especially the ordinary ones that we do every day. These are the most frequent, and therefore upon these, more than upon others, we ought to fix our eyes and to employ our attention and diligence."

~St. Alphonsus Rodriguez

Pray

Show me the good I can attain by giving my work to you, O Lord. Even the mundane little jobs I do every day. Remind me that every small sacrifice has infinite worth when done for you with love.

Act

Be sneaky and do someone else's chores today—all of them. Try not to get caught.

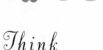

Think

"True poverty of spirit . . . means being at rest in labors and dryness and not seeking consolation or comfort in prayer . . . but seeking consolation in trials for love of him who always lived in the midst of them."

~St. Teresa of Avila

Pray

Today, Lord, I am listening and not talking while I pray. Open my ears, open my heart, and help me to hear you.

Act

Make a simple meal and deliver it to someone you know is lonely or struggling.

Think

"Yes, little and good, this is the best. Therefore, if we wish to advance, or when we wish to give some special honor to our Lord, we have to redouble not our exercises, but the perfection with which we perform them."

~St. Francis de Sales

Pray

I get carried away at times, God, and want to "impress" you with my sacrifices. When I make big plans for giving up and doing more, though, I often fall short of my goals. Help me to remember that doing small things with great love is infinitely more valuable.

Act

Drink only water today. Offer this small sacrifice for those people who have no access to clean drinking water.

Courage

Think

"Stop entertaining those vain fears. Remember it is not feeling which constitutes guilt but the consent to such feelings. Only the free will is capable of good or evil. But when the will sighs under the trial of the tempter and does not will what is presented to it, there is not only no fault but there is virtue."

~ST. PADRE PIO

Pray

Dear God, fear creeps in and quickly robs me of my peace. Strengthen me and help me not to allow fear to take up residence in my heart. Remind me that if I have faith, there is no fear.

Act

Help a child do something today that you previously thought he was too young to do.

APRIL 2

Think

"In this holy abandonment springs up that beautiful free-dom of spirit which the perfect possess, and in which there is found all the happiness that can be desired in this life; for in fearing nothing and seeking and desiring nothing of the things of the world, they possess all."

~St. Teresa of Avila

Pray

Sometimes I am afraid to know your will, God. I am afraid it will be too hard for me. Give me the strength I need to overcome my fears and truly know and do your will in all things.

Act

Do you avoid confession? Get over your jitters and make an appointment to receive healing graces in the sacrament of Reconciliation today.

Think

"Hold your eyes on God and leave the doing to him. That is all the doing you have to worry about."

~St. Jane Frances de Chantal

Pray

Offer a decade of the Rosary today for the intention of being God's instrument.

Act

Wear a cross around your neck or a rosary bracelet on your wrist. When you are fearful or overwhelmed by the duties of your vocation, touch the crucifix or finger the beads. Pray that you can be both courageous and humble enough to leave the doing to God.

Think

"Your reward in heaven will make up completely for all your pain and suffering."

~St. John Bosco

Pray

If any suffering should be required of me today, God, help me to keep my eyes on you and endure all for love of you.

Act

Take a risk today to bring Christ to someone else. Write a letter to the editor of a newspaper, befriend a stranger, or speak out about your faith in a public place.

APRIL 5

Think

"Let the storm rage and the sky darken—not for that shall we be dismayed. If we trust as we should in Mary, we shall recognize in her the Virgin Most Powerful, "who with virginal foot did crush the head of the serpent.""

~POPE ST. PIUS X

Pray

Blessed Mother, when the storms rage around me, it is easy to be swept up in fear. Remind me that I love storms. I love the excitement of rain pounding the roof and the pavement. I love the wind and the crash of thunder. In all the storms of my life, I see God's power and majesty and your tender care. Remind me, Mother, to trust that I am loved and cared for.

Act

Polish your furniture or scrub your floors today. Rub hard. Inhale the scent of cleanliness. Whatever might be worrying you today, push away the fear and breathe in the goodness of God.

APRIL 6

Think

"That which God commands seems difficult and a burden. The way is rough; you draw back; you have no desire to follow it. Yet do so and you will attain glory."

~St. Anthony Mary Zaccaria

Pray

Humans have a natural aversion to pain and suffering. Give me courage today, Lord, to put you first in every part of my life, even if I fear it might cost me dearly.

Act

Wherever you go today—the park, the grocery store, or the post office—resolve to bring those you meet closer to Christ in some way. Offer a small word of encouragement, a patient example, or an act of generosity.

APRIL 7

Think

"Because of our good Lord's tender love to all those who shall be saved, he quickly comforts them saying, 'The cause of all this pain is sin. But all shall be well, and all manner of thing shall be well.' These words were said so kindly and without a hint of blame. So how unjust it would be for me to blame God for allowing my sin when he does not blame me for falling into it."

~BL. JULIAN OF NORWICH

Pray

Holy Spirit, enable me to make a good examination of my conscience. Show me my faults and my sins and then propel me toward forgiveness in confession.

Act

Have you been to confession recently? What are you afraid of? Take the time to make a thorough examination of your conscience. Write it all down. Go to confession; then take your sins to the Lord. Have the courage to let God forgive you.

April 8

Think

"And in every disappointment, great or small, let your heart fly directly to your dear Savior, throwing yourself in those arms for refuge against every pain and sorrow. Jesus will never leave you or forsake you."

~St. Elizabeth Ann Seton

Pray

Teach me to come to you, Lord, with all my fears and sorrows. In all of my trials, give me confidence in your abundant goodness.

Act

What fears are holding you back from greatness? Write them down, give them to God, and return to your day with courage.

April 9

Think

"My hope is in Christ, who strengthens the weakest by his divine help. I can do all in him who strengthens me. His power is infinite, and if I lean on him, it will be mine. His wisdom is infinite, and if I look to him for counsel, I shall not be deceived. His goodness is infinite, and if my trust is stayed in him, I shall not be abandoned."

~Pope St. Pius X

Pray

Remind me again and again, Lord, that "I have strength for everything through him who empowers me!" (Phil 4:13).

Act

Teach your children the verse above. Then get outside today! Challenge them to climb one limb higher, pump the swing just a little harder, pedal just a little faster. Don't be afraid—let them stretch and soar physically.

Think

"We have only one evil to fear, and that is sin."

~St. Alphonsus Liguori

Pray

It is easy to think that death is the greatest evil. Please God, open my eyes and my understanding that I might learn to fear sin more than death.

Act

Is there a person in your life who makes you nervous or uncomfortable? In your contact with that person, remind yourself that he or she is a child of God and treat him or her with love and respect borne of that dignity, not of fear.

Think

"Go forth in peace, for you have followed the good road. Go forth without fear, for he who created you has made you holy, has always protected you, and loves you as a mother. Blessed be you, my God, for having created me."

~ST. CLARE OF ASSISI

Pray

God, make it very clear to me today what is the good road you have paved for me. Don't let me waste a single moment of this glorious spring day. Help me to do exactly what you would have me do, cheerfully and peacefully.

Act

Have a family meeting today, and make a list of things you'd like to do this summer. Put the list in a safe place, and begin working toward making those things happen.

Think

"We've had enough of exhortations to be silent! Cry out with a hundred thousand tongues. I see that the world is rotten because of silence."

~ST. CATHERINE OF SIENA

Pray

I am silent too often, Lord, because I don't want to offend, because I don't want to argue, and because I just want to fit in. Keep me mindful of the times when justice requires that the truth be spoken, and give me courage to do the speaking.

Act

Speak up! Is there a family member or acquaintance who continually speaks falsely or unfairly in your presence? Stop biting your tongue and speak the truth—with charity and love.

Think

"In dangers, in doubts, in difficulties, think of Mary, call upon Mary. With her for guide, you shall never go astray; while invoking her, you shall never lose heart; so long as she is in your mind, you are safe from deception; while she holds your hand, you cannot fall; under her protection you have nothing to fear; if she walks before you, you shall not grow weary; if she shows you favor, you shall reach the goal."

~St. Bernard of Clairvaux

Pray

Blessed Mother, there are women all over the world and women in my neighborhood who awoke today overcome by their fears. Please go to them. Bring them peace. And show me how I can be an instrument of that peace to other women in my life today.

Act

Many women delay doctor's appointments or regular health screenings because they are afraid. Call a friend today and, together, schedule appointments you need to make. Afterward, have a girls' lunch to celebrate.

Think

"Three things can lead us close to God. They are painful physical suffering, being in exile in a foreign land, and being poor by choice because of love for God."

~ST. JUDITH OF PRUSSIA

Pray

God, help me to see suffering as something that can bring me closer to you, instead of something to be avoided at all costs—even sin.

Act

Be unafraid to be "that parent." If there is something from which you feel the need to protect your children, just say no. Even if it might challenge other parents' decisions and even if your children tell you they might die of embarrassment. They will survive. And so will you.

Think

"Whatever troubles may be before you, accept them bravely, remembering whom you are trying to follow. Do not be afraid. Love one another, bear with one another, and let charity guide you all your life. God will reward you as only he can."

~BL. MARY MACKILLOP

Pray

Blessed Mother, show me today the person in my life most in need of an obvious sign of my love. Show me what and how to do whatever it is that will bless them with charity.

Act

Spend several minutes in prayer this morning, asking specifically whom and how to love today. Be obedient to the inspiration of the Holy Spirit.

Think

"Our Lord wills that you cling to him alone! If your faith were greater, how much more peaceful you would be, even when great trials surround and oppress you."

~St. Paula Frassinetti

Pray

Lord, I sometimes feel overwhelmed by my responsibilities and fear for the future of my family. Help me to give over those fears and worries to you, my all-powerful and ever-living God.

Act

Many people ignore financial problems out of fear. Along with your husband, take a close look at your family's finances. Enlist professional help if you need to do so. Add up your debts, and come up with a sound budget plan to pay off debts and work toward financial goals for your future.

Think

"Pray, hope, and don't worry. Worry is useless. God is merciful and will hear your prayer."

~St. Padre Pio

Pray

Sweet Jesus, help me to replace the fearful conversation I have inside my head with constant prayer. Whenever I fall into my old habit of worrying interiorly, nudge me. Remind me to put it all in your hands instead.

Act

Copy the quote above and put it in an obvious place where it will remind you not to let worry run around inside your head. Pray! Pray! Pray instead!

Think

"If the heart wanders or is distracted, bring it back to the point quite gently and replace it tenderly in its Master's presence."

~St. Francis de Sales

Pray

O God, even among the many trials and distractions that will fill my day today, keep my heart focused on you. Remind me that you, who are all-loving, all-knowing, and all-powerful, will be my strength when I am weak.

Act

Have you been avoiding the bathroom scale out of fear? Knowledge is power. Step on it today, and if you see a too-high number, enlist God's help in achieving better health. Make a sound plan for giving up some of your bad habits, eating well, and moving more.

APRIL 19

Think

"The longer the trial to which God subjects you, the greater the goodness in comforting you during the time of the trial and in the exaltation after the combat."

~St. Padre Pio

Pray

Dear Lord, no matter the trial in my life, grant me the blessing of knowing that your grace is sufficient. Let me see that you are always with me, and I will always have the grace and the strength I need.

Act

Write an encouraging note to someone who is suffering. Remind her that you are praying for her. Mail it or deliver it in person today.

APRIL 20

Think

"You—if you are an apostle—will not have to die. You will move to a new house, that's all."

~St. Josemaria Escriva

Pray

I am afraid of death, God. I long to accept my own death, whenever and however you have ordained it to come for me. Give me courage to do that.

Act

Deal with the practical aspects of your own inevitable death today. Make a will that designates caregivers for your children in the event of your death. Even if you can't afford to hire a lawyer, make sure your family knows your wishes with regard to end-of-life care, organ donation, cremation, and burial, too.

April 21

Think

"*Keep close to the Catholic Church at all times, for the Church alone can give you true peace, since she alone possesses Jesus, the true Prince of Peace, in the Blessed Sacrament.*"

~St. Padre Pio

Pray

Remind me, Jesus, that you gave us the Church. Don't allow me to let it be a gift I never fully open. Inspire me and encourage me to learn more every day about the riches of the Church.

Act

Visit a Catholic church with an adoration chapel today. Bring your fears before the Blessed Sacrament. Leave them there.

April 22

Think

"When shall we cast ourselves undeservedly into the arms of our most loving Father in Heaven, leaving to him the care of ourselves and of our affairs, and reserving only the desire of pleasing him, and of serving him well in all that we can?"

~St. Jane Frances de Chantal

Pray

My sweet Jesus, I want to trust in you completely. Help me rid my soul of all nagging fears and doubts. Make me truly your child, free from fear and all anxiety.

Act

Don't worry about looking foolish, and learn something new today. Sign up for a French class, or teach yourself to ride a skateboard or play the guitar. Give up self-consciousness and embrace the whole person God intends you to be.

Think

"Fear not, because God is with you."

~St. Padre Pio

Pray

Enough navel gazing! Lift my chin, God, and focus my eyes on you. Let me take all the little anxieties of my day and all the big fears of my sleepless nights and see them for what they are: a chance for the devil to monopolize the conversation inside my head. I don't want him in my head, God. I want you there. Please be with me.

Act

Is there someone you'd like to get to know better, but you don't follow up on the impulse because you're just a little shy? Be bold! Strike up a conversation; offer an invitation for a cup of coffee. Instead of thinking about yourself, think about making your new friend feel comfortable and welcomed.

Think

"All my life I have wanted to be a missionary. I have wanted to carry the gospel message to those who have never heard of God and the kingdom he has prepared for them."

~Bl. Junipero Serra

Pray

God, I sometimes hold myself back from witnessing to your truth out of fear. I don't want others to think I am silly or pushy or stupid. Help me see that my reluctance robs others of the chance of knowing you. Open my heart and open my lips to bear witness to your truth.

Act

Do something! We all know people living out lives in sin and error. Remind yourself that they are the victims of lies and that you owe them at least an attempt at giving them the truth. Even if you are certain they will reject you, speak the truth in all charity and without fear.

April 25

Think

"Who can assure us that we will be alive tomorrow? Let us listen to the voice of our conscience, to the voice of the royal prophet: 'Today, if you hear God's voice, harden not your heart.' Let us not put off from one moment to another [what we should do] because the [next moment] is not yet ours."

~St. Padre Pio

Pray

So many times, Jesus, I have a good idea, but then I push it aside or procrastinate until the opportunity is gone. Teach me to recognize your whisperings in those good ideas, and give me the nudge I need to act upon them.

Act

Don't let May 1 catch you by surprise! With your children, make paper cones from scrapbook paper and attach a ribbon so that they can be hung on a doorknob. Fill them with silk or paper flowers and a holy card. Now you have May baskets, ready to herald the month of Our Lady!

Think

"The only reason for my being killed is that I have taught the doctrine of Christ. I thank God it is for this reason that I die."

~St. Paul Miki

Pray

Remind me, O God, that there are greater evils than death. Give me strength in my faith so that I might never deny you, even under pain of death.

Act

Many mothers are excessively fearful for their children's physical well-being. Right now, offer to God all the pains, injuries, and illnesses your children might ever suffer for the eternal salvation of their souls.

Think

"When we have once placed ourselves entirely in the hands of God, we need fear no evil. If adversity comes, he knows how to turn it to our advantage, by means which will be in time made clear to us."

~St. Vincent de Paul

Pray

My life is moving at such a frenzied pace. In my fatigue and busyness, I don't always understand your plan, but I am learning that you always have a plan and that your plan is always good. Grant me rest today. I know that if I am well-rested, all my fears seem so much smaller, and you seem so much bigger.

Act

Take a nap today—preferably snuggled close to someone you love.

Think

"The world thrives on lies even twenty centuries after the Truth came among men. We have to tell the truth! This is precisely what we have to do as children of God. When men get used to proclaiming and hearing the truth, there will be more understanding in this world of ours."

~St. Josemaria Escriva

Pray

Give me courage, O Lord, to speak the truth, even when no one wants to hear it.

Act

Are you hiding some personal weakness from your husband out of fear of his judgment? Remember that he is your helpmate to heaven. Open your heart to him in all humility and ask for his help in overcoming your weakness.

APRIL 29

Think

"God never sends us a thorn in our lives that he doesn't send a rose to bloom."

~St. Catherine of Siena

Pray

St. Catherine, today, on your feast day, please pray for me. Pray that I don't become so afraid of the thorns, so concerned about avoiding their sting, that I miss the roses blooming in my life.

Act

This is a good time of year to plant roses! Don't be afraid—roses are increasingly easy to grow. It's impossible to see a blooming rose and not wonder at the beauty of God's creation.

Think

"I had to endure many difficult moments, which I would not wish even on my worst enemies. Nevertheless, I consider my prison days as a higher education in humility. In prison I learned a great many things, as how to be of service to others in their need."

~BL. BASIL HOPKO

Pray

Keep me mindful, dear God, that there are people suffering much greater pains than I am today. Give me courage to face head on all the challenges you will send my way today.

Act

Even if the very idea terrifies you, talk to your kids about sex in whatever way is appropriate for their age level. Do not avoid sharing God's truth with them about this important topic out your own insecurity and fear. Invite them to come to you any time with questions or concerns about their changing bodies, sex, and love.

MAY

Grace

May 1

Think

"Joseph, son of David, do not be afraid to take Mary your wife into your home."

~MATTHEW 1:20

Pray

"O glorious St. Joseph, model of all those who are devoted to labor, obtain for me the grace to work conscientiously, putting the call of duty above my natural inclinations, to work with gratitude and joy, in a spirit of penance for the remission of my sins" (excerpted from the Prayer to St. Joseph the Worker).

Act

What is your work today? Make a list of what you must do. Before you begin, pause to give thanks for work at hand and beg for the grace to do it with joy. Now, go conquer the list!

MAY 2

Think

"*Enlighten our minds, we beseech Thee, O Lord, and impress upon our hearts with the greatness of our loss when we withdraw ourselves from Thee. Grant that we may ever prefer Thee before all things else, and choose rather to lose all worldly goods than relinquish but for one moment Thy grace and love. From henceforth, O Jesus, I desire to die to all things else that I may live only for Thee in time and eternity. Amen.*"

~THOMAS À KEMPIS

Pray

Lord, thank you for sustaining me in all I do. Pour out your graces on my soul and refresh me.

Act

When someone compliments you today or notices something you have accomplished, give the glory to God—both in your heart and in your words.

MAY 3

Think

"Let the soul of Mary be in each of us to magnify the Lord and the spirit of Mary be in each of us to rejoice in God."
~St. Ambrose

Pray

Lord, let me always be mindful of Mary in her home in Nazareth. Give me the grace to be aware of your creative genius and to magnify that in my own home.

Act

Notice the world coming alive this spring. Are there flowers gracing once barren beds of dirt? Our Creator is coloring the world with a magnificent paintbrush. Bring some color into your home today, either with bouquets of flower or little pots of blooming plants. Open the blinds, let in the light. God is beautiful and so is your home!

Think

"With your counsel you guide me, and at the end receive me with honor. Whom else have I in the heavens? None beside you delights me on earth."

~PSALM 73:24–25

Pray

Mother Mary, keep me close to you in all I do. I know that God entrusts you with the task of distributing many of his graces. Fill me where I am empty and make me strong where I am weak.

Act

Plant something today—a whole garden, a bed of flowers, or a small single plant. Remember that just as plants need water and sunshine to thrive and grow, you are dependent upon God's grace.

Think

"All the gifts, virtues, and graces of the Holy Ghost are distributed by Mary, to whom she wishes, when she wishes, the way she wishes and as much as she wishes."

~St. Bernardine of Siena

Pray

Blessed Mother, pray that I will be mindful of my gifts and graces. Ask that I will be blessed with an abundance of gifts, virtues, and graces to use to do God's work here on earth in my sphere of influence.

Act

What gifts, virtues, and graces have you been given? Regift the gifts today in your family. Let those good things about your character—those things which come easily—be an intentional blessing to someone else today. Thank Mary for it.

Think

"Think of what is above, not of what is on earth."

~Colossians 3:2

Pray

I am weak, Lord. I am stubborn, impatient, selfish, and vain. Pour forth your grace to relieve me of my weaknesses. Help me grow strong in virtue.

Act

Think of at least one small flaw in your personality that you tend to make excuses for ("Oh, I've never been a patient person!"), and resolve to work on it with God's help. Decide on a consequence for weakness (doing some small job for each infraction, for example), and then follow through with it.

Think

"There is no sinner in the world, however much he may be at enmity with God, who does not return to him and recover his grace, if he has recourse to [Mary] and asks her assistance."

~St. Bridget of Sweden

Pray

God, I mess up every day. Despite my best intentions, I stumble, fall, and splatter in the muck of sin. Thank you for the gift of example you have given me in the Blessed Mother. Help me to remember daily to ask her assistance in recovering your grace.

Act

Did you mess up somewhere along the way, this first week of May? Did you stumble, fall, and sin somehow, despite your best intentions? Ask Mary to return you to God and make an appointment for confession where you will feel abundant grace poured back into your soul.

MAY 8

Think

"The soul which remains attached to anything, even to the least thing, however many its virtues may be, will never arrive at the liberty of the divine union. It matters little whether a bird be fastened by a stout or slender cord—as long as he does not break it, slender as it may be, it will prevent him from flying freely."

~St. John Chrysostom

Pray

God, show me where I am attached to sin in my life, even small sins. I want to please you with all I do. Give me grace to do that.

Act

Go to Mass or confession or adoration today. Bask in God's graces in the sacraments.

MAY 9

Think

"In the sixth month, the angel Gabriel was sent from God to a town of Galilee called Nazareth, to a virgin betrothed to a man named Joseph, of the house of David, and the virgin's name was Mary. And coming to her, he said, 'Hail, favored one! The Lord is with you.'"

~LUKE 1:26–28

Pray

Lord, let me be still enough to hear when you are calling me. Keep me close to your sacraments and fill my soul with your grace so that I will recognize you in the smallest voices of my day. Give me the grace and strength to always say "Yes" to God's plan for me and mean it.

Act

Does God ever startle you? Are you ever surprised by an inspiration or an idea that just seems like something you couldn't possibly manage on your own? Consider whether it's the prompting of the Holy Spirit. Say "Yes!" and get to it today.

Think

"There is a certain simplicity of heart which is the perfection of all perfections. This is found when our soul fixes her glance solely upon God."

~St. Francis de Sales

Pray

Lord, open my ears to hear your voice in all that I do today. Will you speak to me through a child, through my husband, through a friend, or through a coincidence? Give me grace to hear you.

Act

Spend some time in quiet solitude today, even if just for five minutes. Get up early, stay up a bit at bedtime, or lock yourself in the bathroom if you must. Listen to the quiet and ask God to guide your thoughts.

Think

"As every mandate of grace that is sent by a king passes through the palace gates, so does every grace that comes from Heaven to the world pass through the hands of Mary."

~St. Bernard of Clairvaux

Pray

Blessed Mother, you wait for me, ready to pass the graces of heaven to me in this world. I need those graces! I cannot be the wife or mother or sister or friend I want to be without the grace of God. Open your hands above my head and shower me with the abundant graces of heaven.

Act

Take a walk today. Look at every blooming thing, every splash of color, every leafy tree. See how God has transformed the world this spring. Know that he can take the barren branches of your life and make them blossom with joy. Trust him. Turn your face toward him and let him shower you with grace like a spring rain.

May 12

Think

"We have not received the spirit of the world but the Spirit that is from God, so that we may understand the things freely given us by God."

~1 Corinthians 2:12

Pray

Dear God, thank you for the people you have put in my life, especially friends who share my values and bless me with the gift of good example. Bless all the women in my life today, and give them the grace they need to do your will.

Act

Think of a friend who has been a gift of grace to you in your life. Call her, visit her, or write her a note letting her know the ways in which God has blessed you through her gifts.

Think

"I only ask one grace—may I never offend you."
~ST. THÉRÈSE OF LISIEUX

Pray

Jesus, sometimes my prayers are long and complicated. I know you want to have a conversation with me and I know that you listen no matter how long my list of hopes and wants. Today, though, I come to you with a simple heart. Please grant me the grace today to keep from offending you. Give me the strength and sensitivity to avoid even the near occasion of sin.

Act

Somewhere in your house, create a reminder to ask for grace—painted craft store wooden letters that spell "Grace," an embroidered picture, a small tile painted with the word "Grace" and made into refrigerator magnets. Wander the craft store for inspiration. Pray that your project will bring the whole family greater awareness of grace and of our need to ask for it.

MAY 14

Think

"See how the Blessed Virgin quietly employed one hand in work, while she was holding upon the other arm Our Infant Lord."

~ST. FRANCIS DE SALES

Pray

Mary, I am your child too! Hold me today and give me the strength to do what is right and good.

Act

As you care for the physical needs of children or others today, remember God's tender care for even his smallest children. Hold onto God as you work. Repeat this prayer: "Lord, give me your hands, your eyes, and your heart."

May 15

Think

"He who knows the comforts that come through the gift of grace and knows also how sharp and painful the absence of grace is will not dare think that any goodness comes from himself, but he will openly confess that of himself he is very poor and naked of all virtue."

~Thomas à Kempis

Pray

Show me, Jesus, the work of your hands. Bring me to my knees and give me the words to ask for your grace. Shed light on the dark places of my soul and burn away the muck. Infuse me with your goodness and help me to grow in virtue.

Act

Page through photo albums with a child today. Share with him the moments of grace in your life. Be brave! Talk openly about the times you were afraid and how God brought good out of bad situations. Don't assume your children know the stories. Tell them!

MAY 16

Think

"See why we never arrive at sanctification after so many Communions we make! It is because we do not suffer the Lord to reign in us as he would desire. He enters our breasts and finds our hearts full of desires, affections, and trifling vanities. This is not what he seeks. He would wish to find them quite empty, in order to render himself absolute master and governor of them."

~St. Francis de Sales

Pray

Lord, give me grace to empty myself of all "trifling vanities" and open my heart more fully to you, especially in the sacraments.

Act

Think of a time in your life when you struggled to truly lean on God's grace, during a financial, spiritual, or health crisis. Think of someone you know who might be in a similar situation today and offer her help—even if all you can do is listen to her anxieties and pray for her.

MAY 17

Think

"The profit and increase of spiritual life comes not only when you have devotion but rather when you can humbly and patiently bear the withdrawal and the absence of devotion, yet not cease your prayers or leave undone your other customary good works."

~THOMAS À KEMPIS

Pray

God, sometimes I don't feel moved to pray. You seem very far away and the cares of this world seem so very large. When I get preoccupied, nudge me. Remind me that I exist only because of you and only for you. Let me take those occasions of spiritual dryness and recommit myself to you in the midst of them, knowing that you, like everyone I hold dear, want to talk with me and want me to love you.

Act

God is waiting for you to give him your time and attention. You wouldn't make your child wait if you knew he wanted you. God wants you! Go to him; he is asking for a quantity of your quality time.

Think

"The soul that aims at union with God should value all the operations of his grace, but should only attach itself to that of the present moment."

~Fr. Jean-Pierre de Caussade

Pray

God, I know I have been guilty of worrying excessively about what the future holds. Help me to live one day, one moment at a time, and to find peace in the knowledge that no matter what crises the future holds, your grace will be sufficient.

Act

Write down all your worries and anxieties on a sheet of paper and invite your children to do the same. Pray an Our Father together, noting especially the words "Give us this day our daily bread." Give your worries over to God, and destroy the papers.

May 19

Think

"We should have frequent recourse to prayer, and persevere a long time in it. God wishes to be solicited. He is not weary of hearing us. The treasure of his graces is infinite. We can do nothing more pleasing to him than to beg incessantly that he bestow them upon us."

~St. John Baptist de la Salle

Pray

Dear Lord, I know what it is to hear incessant whining when a child begs. I don't want to whine, God, but I do want to go humbly to you and to ask and ask again for your graces. I want to throw open my heart and to trust that you will take my laundry list of wants and shed your light on them. Transform my litany of desires into a genuine longing to embrace your will for my life.

Act

Today, when a child begs or whines, stop and consider what it is he really desires. Find a way to get to "yes" and grant him what he needs to be happy. He needs you.

Think

"I have sometime placed my hopes in my own virtue, which was no virtue; and when I attempted to run, thinking I was very strong, I fell very quickly and went backward instead of forward. What I expected to reach disappeared, and thus, O Lord, in various ways you have tested my powers."

~St. Augustine

Pray

God, when my life goes smoothly it can be easy to think it's because of my own works and virtues. Help me to see that every good thing I do is a gift of your grace. Remind me of my complete and utter dependence upon you, my Creator and my God.

Act

When you say grace before a meal today, pause to truly consider the meaning of the words you are praying. Talk with your family about where the food you are eating comes from, and point out God's providence in the way the food got from the earth to your table.

Think

"We can never have too much confidence in the good God who is so powerful and so merciful. We obtain from him as much as we hope for."

~St. Thérèse of Lisieux

Pray

God, here are my hopes. I am going to be audacious and list them for you. I am going to ask you to move mightily in my life. And I am going to trust in your power and your mercy.

Act

Make a list today of your hopes. Offer them to God. Put that list somewhere safe. God wants to bless it and you will want to refer to it later.

Think

"First do what's necessary, then do what's possible, and suddenly you are doing the impossible."

~St. Francis of Assisi

Pray

Lord, sometimes I give up too soon, or I fail to even try. I know that all things are possible with you, but help me to truly believe it—so much so that no challenge will seem too great for me to take on.

Act

To what have you said "no" or "I can't" lately? Reconsider. Is there some way, with God's grace, that you can make it happen after all?

MAY 23

Think

"A gracious wife delights her husband, her thoughtfulness puts flesh on his bones; A gift from the Lord is her governed speech, and her firm virtue is of surpassing worth. Choicest of blessings is a modest wife, priceless her chaste person.

Like the sun rising in the Lord's heavens, the beauty of a virtuous wife is the radiance of her home."

~SIRACH 26:1–4, 13–16

Pray

Lord, make of me a holy and decent woman so that I might add grace upon grace to the lives of the people I love.

Act

Your thoughtfulness will put flesh on his bones. What is your husband's favorite dinner? No matter what the trouble, serve that dinner tonight. Set the table with care, prepare plates with an eye toward beauty, and truly enjoy nourishing your family with thoughtfulness.

May 24

Think

"With light from you, I now see that I could not accomplish by myself the things that I wanted to do most. I said to myself: 'I shall do this, I shall finish that,' and I did not do either the one or the other. The will was there but not the power, and if the power was there, my will was not; this because I had trusted in my own strength. Sustain me then, O Lord, for alone I can do nothing. However, when You are my stability, then it is true stability; but when I am my own stability, then it is weakness."

~ST. AUGUSTINE

Pray

God, help me to replace every "I" in my life with you. "God will make the dinner," "God will host a fundraiser," and "God will nurture my children's budding faith." It is only with your help that I can and I will.

Act

Take the children berry picking today or visit a farm stand to buy food for dinner. Note God's bountiful generosity in all the ways he feeds us.

Think

"Clearly, what God wants above all is our will which we received as a free gift from God in creation and possess as though our own. When a man trains himself to act of virtue, it is with the help of grace from God from whom all good things come that he does this. The will is what man has as his unique possession."

~St. Joseph of Cupertino

Pray

Dear Lord, I think of all the things I own and the time and work that have gone into acquiring them, and I wonder: have I spent nearly that time refining my will? My will is the one possession you have given me that is truly unique, and truly valuable. If I can conform my will to yours, I will be happy. The gift of will doesn't have to be dusted, or sorted, or polished, or put away. Help me to use my will only to do what you would have me do.

Act

Today, when a child interrupts you, strengthen your will. Put aside whatever it is you are doing and assent with your whole heart to serve the child in love.

MAY 26

Think

"Cheerfulness strengthens the heart and makes us persevere in a good life. Therefore the servant of God ought always to be in good spirits."

~St. Philip Neri

Pray

God, I am not always naturally in good spirits. Grant me the grace to be cheerful; remind me every moment that I live for you. No matter how dark the day appears, you can and do cheer me. With your grace, I can be in good spirits and I can persevere despite the trials that inevitably will come my way.

Act

Are you grumpy? Ask for grace. Are you tired? Ask for grace. Are you discouraged? Ask for grace. Are you angry? Ask for grace. Be open and yielding and genuinely happy to embrace God's plan. Smile. Let cheerfulness lighten you. If necessary, fake it until it's real.

Think

"If you truly want to help the soul of your neighbor, you should approach God first with all your heart. Ask him simply to fill you with charity, the greatest of all virtues; with it you can accomplish what you desire."

~St. Vincent Ferrer

Pray

Sweet Jesus, sometimes I think that the most difficult aspect of raising children is interacting with all the other adults in their lives: teachers, coaches, doctors, and neighbors. It's so easy to see conflict and contradiction, to wish that we lived in a world of one mind and heart, united with yours. Please help me to love the other adults in my children's lives and to be a loving witness to your goodness and mercy.

Act

Write a sincere thank you note to someone who has touched the life of your child. Mail it.

MAY 28

Think

"*When one has succeeded in placing his heart wholly upon God, he loses his affection for all other things, and no longer finds consolation in anything, nor clings to anything except God.*"

~St. Teresa of Avila

Pray

God, my head and my heart are filled with many things. Some are necessary distractions, but help me to keep focused on you today. You are my Lord and my God who makes all things possible.

Act

Every time you laugh or smile today, say a small prayer of thanks to God for his many blessings. Try to make this a new habit.

Think

"When you think of going to Mass on working days, it is an impulse of the grace that God willed to grant you. Follow it. He did not say ignore it! A saint has told us that one day at Mass he saw Jesus Christ with his hands full of gifts, looking for souls to whom he might give them. But no one was there."

~ST. JOHN VIANNEY

Pray

Jesus, thank you for being available to me in the Eucharist every day. And thank you for allowing me to be with you in spiritual communion when it is truly impossible for me to get to church.

Act

Well now, you just thought of going to Mass on a working day. Go!

Think

"Rather, imitate little children, who with one hand cling to their fathers, while with the other they pluck strawberries and mulberries along the hedges. Attend to what you are doing, yet not without raising a glance from time to time to your Heavenly Father, to see whether he is pleased with your plans and to ask his help."

~St. Francis de Sales

Pray

God, help me to see your providence and guidance in my husband's employment and/or my own. Thank you for the work we do and for the talents and efforts of other people who make it possible.

Act

Pray a decade of the Rosary or offer some small sacrifice for the intentions of someone at your husband's workplace or your own who has been especially helpful to your family. Thank God for the graces that have come to your family through that person's actions.

MAY 31

Think

"You never think of Mary without Mary's thinking of God for you. You never praise or honor Mary without Mary's praising and honoring God with you. If you say 'Mary,' she says 'God.' St. Elizabeth praised Mary, and called her blessed, because she had believed. Mary, the faithful echo of God at once intoned: 'My soul doth magnify the Lord.'"

~St. Louis de Montfort

Pray

God, let me never be too shy or too busy to visit with someone who needs me.

Act

Today, on the Feast of the Visitation, bake a batch of cookies, pack a box of teabags, and plan to go visiting. Or make a meal for a pregnant mom who could use a little unexpected help today. Find the time to visit someone whose load will be lightened by your love.

Gentleness

JUNE 1

Think

"*Grace has five effects in us: first, our soul is healed; second, we will good; third, we work effectively for it; fourth, we persevere; fifth, we break through to glory.*"

~St. Thomas Aquinas

Pray

God, I am greedy for grace. Shower me with the strength I need to be gentle in all things.

Act

Find an online version of "Hail Mary, Gentle Woman" (for example, at SpiritandSong.com). Listen to it every morning this month. Begin your day with this gentle litany.

June 2

Think

"Put your soul every morning in a posture of humility, tranquility, and sweetness, and notice from time to time through the day if it has become entangled in affection for anything; and if it be not quiet, disengaged and tranquil, set it at rest."

~St. Francis de Sales

Pray

Give me your voice today, Mary. May I speak all things in sweetness and love.

Act

What was the last thing you said to someone? Examine the words, the tone, and the gestures you used. Would anyone describe them as gentle? If not, aim for improvement.

JUNE 3

Think

"Since I began to love, love has never forsaken me. It has ever grown to its own fullness within my innermost heart."

~St. Catherine of Genoa

Pray

Dear Lord, thank you for the love of my life. Thank you for the time you have given us to grow together. Please bless us with an appreciation for one another.

Act

June is wedding month! Gather all the wedding pictures from loved ones' weddings and display them somewhere in your home this month. Pray for those marriages every time you see them.

JUNE 4

Think

"The insight of the most skilled doctors can't compare to a mother's heart."

~St. Thérèse of Lisieux

Pray

Lord, keep me mindful of the fact that motherhood is a privilege. Let me never abuse my authority over my children. Keep me forever a source of sweetness in their eyes.

Act

Do not correct any child with a loud voice today. Instead, go to the child in need of discipline, make eye contact, and use a quiet voice to correct him or her. Let your quiet, invested, persistent actions speak volumes of love to your children.

Think

"Give me a heart as big as the universe!"

~St. Frances Cabrini

Pray

Dear God, I want a heart as big as the universe. I want, too, a heart for the universe. You have created a world so full of people and places to love. Help me to cultivate in myself and in my children a love for all your creatures.

Act

Do you have a summer reading plan? As a family, decide on a summer reading incentive program (or sign up for your library's program). Kick off the summer with a trip to the library to gather books. Commit to a regular day and time all summer to exchange the books you've read for new ones. You have the world at your fingertips.

Think

"Great affairs do not disturb us so much as a great number of little ones; therefore, receive these also with calmness, and try to attend to them in order, one after another, without perturbation. Thus, you will gain great merit by them."

~St. Francis de Sales

Pray

Dear Lord, sometimes so many little things add up until I can't seem to control my temper any more. Help me to see these small annoyances for the gifts of grace they can be—if only I will accept them as you send them.

Act

When anyone upsets you with their words or actions today, pause before responding. Breathe a prayer to their guardian angel, asking for grace to respond with gentleness.

Think

"Just as he gives the gardener the skill to tend rare and delicate plants while fertilizing them himself, so he wishes to use others in his cultivation of souls."

~St. Thérèse of Lisieux

Pray

You are the Master Gardener. Help me to be diligent. Teach me to prune and to weed so that my soul bears abundant fruit for you!

Act

Begin a summer art journal with your children. The night before, set the breakfast table with colored pencils, markers, and watercolors. Surprise each child with a new, spiral-bound sketchbook. Start by sketching plants in your yard or your newly-planted garden. Set aside time to update your garden journal once a week.

JUNE 8

Think

"One great means of preserving constant peace and tranquility of heart is to receive all things as coming from the hands of God, whatever they may be, and in whatever way they may come."

~St. Dorotheus

Pray

Help me to see your hand in all that happens to me today, God. Give me serenity to accept the life you have seen fit to give me and the trials you see fit to send me today.

Act

Do some small, slow, deliberate task with your hands—folding laundry, sewing, making bread, dusting bookshelves. Offer each moment of your work in thanksgiving to God for the privilege of blessing your family with your hands.

Think

"You can win more converts with a spoonful of honey than a barrelful of vinegar."

~ST. FRANCIS DE SALES

Pray

Dear Lord, sweeten my tongue. Whenever an acidic comment comes to mind, cover my words with honey. Let me speak kindly and gently and graciously, no matter how I feel inside.

Act

Make a special peach dessert tonight. Dip whole ripe peaches in boiling water for a minute. This will make them easy to peel. Peel and cut them into slices with a sharp knife, drizzle with just a little honey, and serve with freshly whipped cream. Talk about the sweetness of God's goodness and grace.

Think

"Think well. Speak well. Do well. These three things, through the mercy of God, will make a man go to heaven."

~St. Camillus de Lellis

Pray

Lord, in all my thoughts, words, and actions, protect me from the sins of rash judgment and anger. Especially when I am feeling frustrated and wronged, slow me down and keep me cool.

Act

Exercise provides a physical release for stress and frustration. Go for a walk today, ride a bike, race up and down the stairs, or play tag with your kids in the yard.

Think

"My precious children stick to me like little burrs, they are so fearful of losing me again [after a trip]. The moment I shake off one side another clings on the opposite, nor can I write one word without some sweet interruption."

~St. Elizabeth Ann Seton

Pray

God, make me very aware of the fact that my children are always sweet interruptions, especially when it doesn't seem so.

Act

Make play dough today. Add a little lavender oil or vanilla or even a dash of glitter to it to make it look and smell heavenly. Sit and play with it with your children. Resist the urge to leave them to go get something accomplished. If you have no children of play dough age, make a batch and bring it to play with someone else's children. Their mother will be ever so grateful.

Think

"Be kindhearted to the poor, the unfortunate, and the afflicted. Give them as much help and consolation as you can. Thank God for all the benefits he has bestowed upon you, that you may be worthy to receive greater."

~St. Louis IX

Pray

Help me to see who needs me most today, God. I can't be all things to all people, but I can be a means of great grace to one person who needs me most. Point me in that direction.

Act

Have you ever said something and regretted it almost immediately? Don't let that happen today. Think twice, speak once.

JUNE 13

Think

"St. Francis de Sales, that great saint, would leave off writing with the letter of a word half-formed in order to reply to an interruption."

~St. John Vianney

Pray

St. John Vianney, pray for me. Pray that I will always know what my most important work is and that I will be gentle with the people of my vocation and remember that they are God's will for me.

Act

Allow yourself to be interrupted. When someone intrudes upon a thought or an act, stop what you are doing, smile, and look them in the eye. Give them your full, unhurried attention.

June 14

Think

"Christ with me, Christ before me, Christ behind me, Christ within me, Christ below me, Christ above me, Christ at my right, Christ at my left, Christ in lying down, Christ in sitting, Christ in rising up, Christ in the heart of every man who thinks of me, Christ in the mouth of every man who speaks to me, Christ in every eye that sees me, Christ in every ear that hears me."

~St. Patrick

Pray

Jesus, give me your hands, your tongue, and your heart today. Use me to touch and to love precious souls and draw them ever closer to you.

Act

Most of us talk too much. Resolve to speak half as much today as you usually do. Listen more; talk less.

Think

"Do something good for someone you like least today."
~St. Anthony of Padua

Pray

God, there are people in my life who are just plain difficult. Help me to love them. Help me love them well.

Act

Listen to good St. Anthony. Who is the "someone" who will benefit from your love today?

JUNE 16

Think

"*Virtues are formed by prayer. Prayer preserves temperance. Prayer suppresses anger. Prayer prevents emotions of pride and envy. Prayer draws into the soul the Holy Spirit, and raises man to heaven.*"

~St. Ephrem of Syria

Pray

Jesus, meek and humble of heart, make my heart like yours!

Act

Commit the above prayer to memory and recite it as you wash the dishes, do laundry, or any perform any other manual work that leaves your mind free.

Think

"To humble ourselves, to suffer our imperfections with patience, this is true sanctity, the source of peace."

~ST. THÉRÈSE OF LISIEUX

Pray

Blessed Mother, please pray that I will learn to be gentle with myself. Help me to see my imperfections as places where God can make his power perfect in my weakness.

Act

Take an hour for yourself today. Treat yourself kindly: get a pedicure, go read a book in a park, sip iced coffee in an outdoor cafe.

Think

"Never be hurried by anything whatever—nothing can be more pressing than the necessity for your peace before God. You will help others more by the peace and tranquility of your heart than by any eagerness or care you can bestow on them."

~St. Elizabeth Ann Seton

Pray

Lord, give me peace of mind and heart. Give me the grace of seeing the "big picture" so that I might fret less frequently about small things that don't matter.

Act

Give up some computer time, phone calls, or television today to make some extra time for quiet prayer. Give God a chance to speak to your heart and make you temperate, humble, and gentle.

JUNE 19

Think

"No one heals himself by wounding another."

~St. Ambrose

Pray

I promise you today, Lord, that I will do everything in my power to avoid using my words to hurt someone else, even if I've been hurt. Infuse me with your grace and give me the strength I need to keep that promise.

Act

Return an insult with a blessing today.

Think

"If you want someone to love you, you must be the first to love; and if you have nothing to give, give yourself."

~BL. ROSALIE RENDU

Pray

Lord, when I argue with someone, it can be very hard to be the first to give in. Remind me that giving up and giving way are not synonyms for losing, but synonyms for loving.

Act

Think of the last person who wronged you, even if he or she did so in some seemingly insignificant way. Reach out to that person today with a generous spirit of forgiveness and love—do them a favor or speak some kind words. Make your actions a special gift for God.

JUNE 21

Think

"Take shelter under Our Lady's mantle, and do not fear. She will give you all you need. She is very rich, and besides is very generous with her children. She loves giving."

~BL. RAPHAELA MARIA

Pray

Blessed Mother, I want to be like you. I want to be very rich; please ask God for graces on my behalf. I want to be generous with my children. Help me to give without ceasing.

Act

Get to "yes" today. When someone you love asks for something, don't offer a reflexive "no." Find a way to get to "yes" before you respond. Be creative. Be flexible. Be kind. Be willing to give until it hurts.

JUNE 22

Think

"This was the method that Jesus used with the apostles. He put up with their ignorance and roughness and even their infidelity. He treated sinners with a kindness and affection that caused some to be shocked, others to be scandalized, and still others to hope for God's mercy. And so he bade us to be gentle and humble of heart."

~St. John Bosco

Pray

Help me to follow your good example, Jesus. Teach me to treat everyone—especially sinners—with kindness and affection.

Act

Think of someone you know who might need a friend today—someone going through marital troubles, suffering financial problems, or struggling with an addiction. Go to that person today and be the Body of Christ to him or her.

JUNE 23

Think

"They [your critics] are the losers; they lose interior joy, for there is nothing sweeter than to think well of one's neighbor."

~St. Thérèse of Lisieux

Pray

Dear Lord, how often have I lost interior joy by giving in to the dialogue in my head that argues with my neighbors? Still my interior voice. Replace my racing thoughts with peace. Grant me the sweetness of truly seeing you in everyone I meet.

Act

Is there a neighbor in your life who makes you uncomfortable? Sweeten things up. Bake cookies for that person today.

Think

"All our religion is but a false religion, and all our virtues are mere illusions, and we ourselves are only hypocrites in the sight of God, if we have not that universal charity for everyone—for the good, and for the bad, for the poor and for the rich, and for all those who do us harm as much as those who do us good."

~St. John Vianney

Pray

Grant me grace to see others as you see them, Lord. Help me to see the precious soul beneath even the worst kinds of sinners. Take my words and actions today and make them gifts of grace for someone in need.

Act

Think of someone who serves you but with whom you don't have a personal relationship—a bank teller, a store clerk, a police officer, or a doctor. Give that person a small gift today with a note thanking them for the gift of their service.

June 25

Think

"Make many acts of love, for they set the soul on fire and make it gentle."

~St. Teresa of Avila

Pray

Open my eyes wide, dear Lord. Let me see all those small acts of love for which you created me. I want to be your instrument. Show me where to go and what to do.

Act

Buy some very small silk flowers (three inches high or so). Set them in your family room or on your kitchen table in front of a glass bowl. For every act of love, invite your children to put a flower in the bowl. When the bowl is full, make small bouquets of the silk flowers and tie them with thin ribbon. Put the bouquet in front of statues of Mary you have in your home or take them to church and offer them to Mary there.

JUNE 26

Think

"In everything, whether it is a thing sensed or a thing known, God himself is hidden within."

~St. Bonaventure

Pray

Dear God, help me to see Jesus Christ in all others who cross my path today. Give me the grace I need to treat all those made in your image with charity, respect, and dignity.

Act

Mind your thoughts as well as your words today. Do not allow yourself to think things you would not say out loud.

June 27

Think

"Walk with simplicity in the way of the Lord and do not torment your spirit. Learn to hate your faults, but to hate them calmly."

~St. Padre Pio

Pray

St. Padre Pio, you never cease to make me smile. Pray that I can, indeed, hate with calmness. I want to rid myself of my own faults, to rout them out with gentle ferocity. My children, too, have faults. It is ever so important that I hate those with a gentle demeanor, too. Help me to do it with gentle patience and loving kindness.

Act

When you correct today, do so with extreme care for gentleness. Let your posture and your tone reflect calm.

Think

"The perfection of souls, and the degree of excellence to which they have attained, can be gauged by their fidelity to the order established by God."

~Fr. Jean-Pierre de Caussade

Pray

Heal my heart of all bitterness, Lord. Help me to let go of all the hurt and anger from my past. I forgive all. I give all.

Act

Admit that you are holding a grudge against someone, even someone you have already reconciled with and even if it is only in your heart. Write down your grudge, give it to God in thanksgiving for the mercy he has shown you, and then destroy the paper you have written it on.

Think

"While some women exalt in the management of their households and other in piety—for it is difficult to achieve both—[St. Nonna] surpassed all in both. She increased the resources of her household by her care and practical foresight. . . . She devoted herself to God as one removed from household cares."

~St. Gregory Nazianzen

Pray

Dear God, I can't help but sigh when I read about St. Nonna. I want to be an excellent wife. I want to manage my household well. Most of all, I want to be holy. Please God, let me grow in my multitasking. Give me the gift of acquiring holiness while managing my home.

Act

As you move through your house today, attending to all those things which are your duty, sing. If you're inspired to sing hymns of praise, all the better. But if all you can manage are Disney tunes, that's fine, too. Bring gentle joy to your work.

Think

"The will of God in the present moment is the source of sanctity."

~Fr. Jean-Pierre de Caussade

Pray

Sometimes I don't want to know your will, God. I want to focus only on my own. Make me humble, gentle, and submissive to all that you would have me do.

Act

Refuse to say anything negative today. If you must correct someone, find a pleasant, positive way of phrasing the correction.

JULY

Humility

July 1

Think

"Acknowledge that without Me you can do nothing, but I will never let you lack help as long as you keep your weakness and nothingness buried in My strength."

~St. Margaret Mary Alacoque

Pray

Lord, remind me today how small I am. Help me to see that I am nothing without you.

Act

Think of a small but necessary task you usually avoid because of its unpleasantness. Remind yourself of the fact that Jesus washed his disciples' feet and do that task today out of love and service for others.

Think

"Do not let any occasion of gaining merit pass without taking care to draw some spiritual profit from it; as, for example, from a sharp word which someone may say to you; from an act of obedience imposed against your will; from an opportunity which may occur to humble yourself, or to practice charity, sweetness, and patience. All of these occasions are gain for you."

~St. Ignatius Loyola

Pray

On this day, Lord, help me to be mindful of you. Whenever I am annoyed or inconvenienced or insulted or injured, help me to see that these things are for my benefit. Give me grace to conform my will to yours and respond as you would; bring my soul ever closer to your heart.

Act

Surprise your husband by cleaning out his car. Go all out and vacuum and spray all the seats with something that smells nice. Tape a love note to the steering wheel. Take joy in knowing that you were able to turn a mess into something sweet.

Think

"I know, O my God, that you put hearts to the test and that you take pleasure in uprightness. With a sincere heart I have willingly given all these things, and now with joy I have seen your people here present also giving to you generously."

~1 Chronicles 29:17

Pray

Make me small and humble today, Lord. I want to serve you as even your smallest creatures do.

Act

Is there someone who belittles you? Offer your chores today for that person's intentions.

JULY 4

Think

"The wise man should show his wisdom not by his eloquence but by good works; the humble man should not proclaim his own humility, but leave others to do so and recognize that the ability to control their desires has been given them by another. To him be glory for ever and ever."
~Pope St. Clement I

Pray

God, guard my tongue. Give me the grace to keep quiet when my first impulse is to talk. Help me to see that I don't have to express an opinion or even share my knowledge on everything.

Act

Consciously choose not to speak about something today. Instead, do something that serves someone else. Don't stew about what you could have or should have said—smile instead.

July 5

Think

"For in a severe test of affliction, the abundance of their joy and their profound poverty overflowed in a wealth of generosity on their part."

~2 Corinthians 8:2

Pray

Lord, help me to see the value in quietly offering my sufferings to you. Give me grace to silently and gratefully accept my circumstances.

Act

If there is something in your home or family that you feel like complaining about today, keep quiet. Know that God knows your complaint already and has seen fit to let it be. Hold your tongue and thank God for the opportunity to grow.

Think

"Consider seriously how quickly people change, and how little trust is to be had in them; and hold fast to God, who does not change."

~St. Teresa of Avila

Pray

God, save me from putting my faith in other people. Instead, let me put my faith in you. Help me to recognize that my husband is the only person bound to me by a covenant with you. No one else holds that place in my life. Remind me to turn first to you, and then to him.

Act

Today, when you are tempted to pick up the phone and chat with a friend, call your husband instead. Just check in on his day and remind him you love him. When he is home and away from work, give him your full attention and the full sharing of your heart. Invest more time and attention to this sacramental relationship than you do to any other earthly relationship.

Think

"But I am afraid that, as the serpent deceived Eve by his cunning, your thoughts may be corrupted from a sincere (and pure) commitment to Christ."

~2 CORINTHIANS 11:3

Pray

My mind is filled with many worldly cares, God. Remind me today that I need nothing more than you. If I am poor and lowly with you, it is enough.

Act

Set a timer to go off at regular intervals today (every hour or every three hours, depending upon your schedule). Every time it rings, whatever you are doing, pause and refocus your attention on God, giving thanks for his grace and guidance in all things.

July 8

Think

"Wisdom enters through love, silence, and mortification. It is great wisdom to know how to be silent and to look at neither the remarks, nor the deeds, nor the lives of others."

~St. John of the Cross

Pray

God, I get so discouraged sometimes. I compare myself to my friends and all I see is my lacking. Help me to narrow my view and look instead at the blessings of talent, treasure, life, and love that you have given specifically to me. Be with me this day and show me how you would have me use those gifts.

Act

Is there something you read that causes you to doubt yourself or question your worth? A magazine, a blog, or a book that makes you despair? Promise yourself and God that you will fast from that particular thing for the rest of this month.

JULY 9

Think

"God is a Being most simple in his essence, admitting no composition whatever. If, then, we desire to render ourselves as much like him as possible, we should endeavor to be by virtue what he is by nature."

~St. Vincent de Paul

Pray

Lord, free me from those things that are obstacles toward my greater holiness—pride, fear, and worldly concerns. Make me more aware of my dependence upon you in all things.

Act

Call a friend or anyone you know who is struggling in some way. Don't talk; just listen.

Think

"Love is the genuine fruit of prayer when prayer is rooted in humility."

~St. Teresa of Avila

Pray

Jesus, I come before you today on my knees. I know, with all my heart, that I am nothing without you. Every good thing I can be, every good thing I can do, I can only be or do with your grace. Infuse me with your spirit and crowd out every last bit of my pride. Show me, with crystal clarity, whom and how you would have me love today.

Act

Sit quietly for fifteen minutes today after reading the quote and the prayer above. Focus on Jesus. In your mind, see him loving the people of his hidden life in Nazareth. Let him show you who needs your love today.

JULY 11

Think

"With those who are perfect and walk with simplicity, there is nothing small and contemptible, if it be a thing that pleases God; for the pleasure of God is the object at which alone they aim, and which is the reason, the measure, and the reward of all their occupations, actions and plans; and so, in whatever they find this, it is for them a great and important thing."

~St. Alphonsus Rodriguez

Pray

God, show me my pride in all its ugliness. Open my heart to hear the exact ways in which you are calling me to give up habits of vanity and selfishness. Give me strength to overcome them.

Act

Everyone owes someone an apology, even if only for long-ago offenses. Apologize today with no "ifs" or "buts."

JULY 12

Think

"We certainly are sparks! This is why you want us to humble ourselves. Just as sparks receive their being from the fire, so let us acknowledge that our being comes from our first source."

~ST. CATHERINE OF SIENA

Pray

I am creative, just as you are my Creator, Lord. Sometimes, my life seems monotonous and I can't see the sparks. Light a fire in my soul, God, and show me how you want me to be creative in my domestic church.

Act

Build a fire (or light the grill) and make s'mores tonight.

Think

"Simplicity ought to be held in great esteem. . . . it is a virtue most worthy of love, because it leads us straight to the Kingdom of God."

~St. Vincent de Paul

Pray

Lord, help me to see that you are in all the tiny tasks that make up my days. Help me to find you and embrace you in even the very small and hidden parts of my vocation.

Act

Clean a hidden space today—a closet, a cabinet, behind the couches, a DVD drawer, an email inbox, or a buried bookshelf. Make it a perfect hidden gift for God and your family.

July 14

Think

"Nothing can disturb us but self-love and the importance we give ourselves. If we are without feelings of tenderness and compassion in our heart, have no delight or devotion in prayer and no interior sweetness in meditation, we fall into sadness; if we have difficulty in doing things well, or if something gets in the way of our plans, at once we are anxious to overcome it and fret about getting rid of it."

~St. Francis de Sales

Pray

There are days, sweet Jesus, when I feel like everything gets in the way of my plans. I am tired. I am frustrated and discouraged. Divert my attention from myself, and help me devote myself to sweet meditation.

Act

The first time you are interrupted today, set aside whatever it was you were doing and look your interrupter in the eyes. Listen carefully to what he or she has to say and respond promptly and with all the love and patience of the Blessed Mother.

Think

"God loves the simple and converses with them willingly and communicates to them the understanding of his truths, because he disposes of these at his pleasure. He does not deal thus with lofty and subtle spirits."

~St. Francis de Sales

Pray

I know the value of rote prayers, God, but it's sometimes easy to lose myself and become distracted when reciting from memory. Help me to also make a habit of using my own simple voice to speak directly to you throughout my days.

Act

Write the words "small," "little," "meek," and "humble" on cards and leave them where you will see them today. Each time you see one, remember that you are small, and offer a prayer to God asking for the virtue of humility.

Think

"How happy I am to see myself imperfect and be in need of God's mercy."

~St. Thérèse of Lisieux

Pray

I notice, Jesus, how ugly some kinds of herbs are. If I didn't know better, I'd take them for weeds. And yet, they were all created by you for a useful purpose and many of them taste and smell sweet and beautiful. When I see only my ugliness and my imperfections, Lord, show me your vision for me.

Act

Make herbal honey today. Put an inch or so of good quality honey in a jar and then put some aromatic herbs over it (thyme, bee balm, or mint are good choices). Pour more honey over the herbs and continue to layer all the way up the jar. Cover and let sit for a few weeks. Reflect on the sweetness of God's mercy.

JULY 17

Think

"The very deficiency of material things enhances, increases, and enriches the faith: the less for the eyes, the more for the soul."

~Fr. Jean-Pierre de Caussade

Pray

God, open my eyes and my heart to the ways I seek to build myself up with material possessions, recognition, and status. Make me ever more aware of the vanity of earthly glories.

Act

Children are brutally honest. Ask one of your children today how he or she thinks you could be a better mother. Listen to the answers with an open mind and a spirit of humility.

JULY 18

Think

"To be taken with love for a soul, God does not look on its greatness, but the greatness of its humility."

~St. John of the Cross

Pray

Humble, humble, humble! I make grand plans, God, and I think I can do all sorts of big things. How long will it take me to remember that you don't want my lists of grand plans? Show me what you would have me do today and slow me to walk with you instead of barreling ahead on my own steam.

Act

Go to a farmer's market today. Slow down and take time to notice how beautiful the food is and how enticing it smells. Gather up some humble fruits and vegetables and then go home and bless your family with a feast of God's goodness.

Think

"The greatest fault among those who have a good will is that they wish to be something they cannot be, and do not wish to be what they necessarily must be. They conceive desires to do great things for which, perhaps, no opportunity may ever come to them, and meantime neglect the small which the Lord puts in their hands."

~St. Francis de Sales

Pray

Lord, give me grace to see the small parts of my duties that I might be neglecting. I want to attend to these today.

Act

In conversations today, when tempted to share something about yourself or your accomplishments, keep quiet. Listen to others' input and give thanks to God for all their gifts instead.

Think

"You will not see anyone who is really striving after his advancement who is not given to spiritual reading. And as to him who neglects it, the fact will soon be observed by his progress."

~St. Athanasius

Pray

Jesus, what would you have me read this summer? Guide me in my choice and help me to stick to a reading plan.

Act

Go to a Catholic bookstore and ask the clerk for advice on spiritual reading. Trust that the Holy Spirit will guide your selection. Commit yourself to fifteen minutes of spiritual reading at a designated time for the rest of the summer.

Think

"In my little way, there are only ordinary things."

~St. Thérèse of Lisieux

Pray

Lord, help me to see that my own sanctity lies in embracing the little things you send my way—small sacrifices and tiny crosses.

Act

Commit to saying only "yes" to God today. Hear his voice commanding you to be faithful in every small chore or unpleasant circumstance that falls in your path today, and aim to answer "Yes, Lord!" immediately and with joy.

JULY 22

Think

"The proud person is like a grain of wheat thrown into water: it swells, it gets big. Expose that grain to the fire: it dries up, it burns. The humble soul is like a grain of wheat thrown into the earth: it descends, it hides itself, it disappears, it dies; but to revive in heaven."

~BL. MARY OF JESUS CRUCIFIED

Pray

Pray the Litany of Humility today: Jesus, give me a humble heart like your own. Turn my selfish desires into selfless ones and help me to see your face in everyone I meet.

Act

What's the most distasteful job in your house? Cleaning up the dog droppings in the backyard? Scrubbing the gunk from behind the toilet? Sweeping the garage? Whatever it is, do it. While you work, give thanks for the blessings in your life.

July 23

Think

"Be not of those who think perfection consists in under-taking many things, but of those who place it in doing well what little they do. For it is much better to do little and to do it well, than to undertake much and do it ill."

~St. Francis de Sales

Pray

Lord, even in the summertime, family life can feel so busy. Help me to slow down today and savor the small joys that are part of my daily duties—the smell of flowers, the sweetness of a child's smile, warm sunshine, and days outdoors.

Act

Remove something from your to-do list today. Replace it with time you spend with your children— reading to them, talking with them, or enjoying the outdoors together.

Think

"Humility does not disturb or disquiet however great it may be; it comes with peace, delight, and calm. . . . The pain of genuine humility doesn't agitate or afflict the soul; rather, this humility expands it and enables it to serve God more."

~ST. TERESA OF AVILA

Pray

God, help me to see the great freedom that comes with humility. You make me who I am. I don't need to worry that I will not be good enough, smart enough, or competent enough. All I need to be is what you made me to be. And that will be enough.

Act

Do something nice for yourself today: give yourself a manicure, buy fresh fruit at the farmer's market, drink a cup of iced tea at an outdoor cafe. Whatever it is that awakens your senses and refreshes your soul, make some time for that today. Revel a bit in the way God made you.

Think

"If we care nothing for any created things, but embrace the Creator alone, His Majesty will infuse the virtues into us in such a way that, provided we labor to the best of our abilities day by day, we shall not have to wage war much longer."

~St. Teresa of Avila

Pray

Lord, help me to see that my work in my home is not meant to be a means of showing off to others ("See how clean I keep my bathroom!" or "See what a talented cook I am!") but a means of serving my family.

Act

Invite a friend over for lunch or an iced tea today, but do not scramble to clean the house top to bottom before she arrives. Be humble enough to enjoy her company and offer hospitality without concern for appearances.

JULY 26

Think

"Let us do three things, my dearest daughter, and we shall have peace: let us have a very pure intention of seeking, in all things, the honor and glory of God; let us do the little we can toward this end according to the advice of our spiritual father; and let us leave to God the care of all the rest."

~St. Jane Frances de Chantal

Pray

Pray a St. Anne chaplet today for the intention of the three things above. If possible, pray that chaplet in church after spiritual direction and confession.

Act

Consider making a St. Anne chaplet to keep at hand (see "Tutorial for St. Anne Chaplet" at gardensofgrace .net). This is a beautiful devotion that is so easy to incorporate into daily life. Even if you don't make the chaplet, this devotion is easy to count on your fingers.

JULY 27

Think

"Be careful not to forget God in your occupations, from a belief that in this way you will accomplish more; for if He abandons you, you will not be able to take a step without falling prostrate on the ground."

~St. Francis de Sales

Pray

Dear God, sometimes I think that if I have to fold another load of laundry, plan another meal, or wipe another bottom, my brain will begin oozing from my ears. Remind me of the heavy cross you carried for love of us and help me to commit anew to working at even the most menial tasks required of my vocation.

Act

Write the word "God" on at least a dozen small pieces of paper and ask your kids to hide them places you might find them throughout the day—in the pantry, in the laundry, near the phone. Whenever you find one, remember that God truly is hidden in all the corners of your home and all the little things you do each day.

July 28

Think

"If your enemies see that you grow courageous, and that you will neither be seduced by flatteries nor disheartened by the pains and trials of your journey, but rather are contented with them, they will grow afraid of you."

~Bl. Henry Suso

Pray

God, there are people in my life who seem to delight in my stumbling. Make me ever mindful that it is in making mistakes that I grow. Let me smile from the ground and lift my head to see you help me up. Please, Jesus, make of me a good witness to your graciousness.

Act

When you make a mistake with your children today (and you will), admit it, and apologize sincerely. Say it all out loud, and make sure they understand that God uses these instances to refine your soul and draw you closer to him.

Think

"How can the sun and moon praise God, as the Prophet exhorts them to? By performing well that task which has been imposed on them by the Lord. This is great praise which they give him. Behold, then, an excellent way in which you can praise God at all times—by performing well your tasks and whatever you may have to do."

~St. Jerome

Pray

Lord, sometimes it feels as if all depends upon me— the housework, the shopping, the phone calls, and the meals. Help me to see that all really depends on you, and that none of us is anything without you.

Act

Spend some time today outdoors, alone, or with your family. Notice how even a plant or a tiny bug gives God glory with its obedience to its nature. Give thanks to God for your own "nature" and pray to know it more completely.

July 30

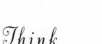

Think

"And since pride blinds us, impoverishes us, and dries us up by robbing us of the richness of grace, it leaves us unfit to govern ourselves or anyone else."

~St. Catherine of Siena

Pray

God, sometimes I think that I am so much wiser than my children. Really, though, my soul is scarred by years of pride. Help me to be more like the children in my life—fully open to your goodness and your grace, fully confident that you will care for me.

Act

Act like a child today—go to the pool and really play; go to the park and slide down the slide; go to the beach and build sand castles. Do something that allows you to frolic in the sunshine (or the rain) with your children today. Let them teach you to play.

Think

"Whatever you do, do from the heart, as for the Lord and not for others."

~COLOSSIANS 3:23

Pray

Lord, sometimes even my very best efforts and sacrifices go unrecognized. No one notices the laundry, child care, or other housework unless it doesn't get done. Help me to lose my attachment to recognition and perform my work and acts of service out of love for you alone.

Act

Invite your children to help you with a household chore today. Don't be afraid to let them know that you need help and that it's okay to ask for help in life. No one is perfect, and nothing needs to be perfect to be pleasing to God.

AUGUST

Charity

AUGUST 1

Think

"Love! love! love! my daughters; I know nothing else."
~St. Jane Frances de Chantal

Pray

God, help me to bring your love to everyone I meet today. Let all that I think, speak, and do be rooted in the eternal love that comes only from you.

Act

Remember we are called to love others, even when we don't "like" them. Make a mental list of people you have trouble loving. Add their intentions to your prayer list for this month.

Think

"When the love of God obtains the mastery of a soul, it produces in it an insatiable desire to labor for the Beloved; so that, though it may perform many and great works and spend much time in his service, all seems nothing, and it constantly grieves at doing so little for its God, and if it could annihilate itself and perish for him, it would be well pleased."

~St. John Chrysostom

Pray

Dear Lord, I work to serve the people you have given me to love, but some days, I look around and all I can see is how much more I could do. On those days, please console me and inspire me. Give me the strength of your grace to keep laboring for you.

Act

Buy a pack of bathtub crayons. Surprise someone with love notes.

Think

"Simplicity is nothing but an act of charity, pure and simple, which has but one sole end—that of gaining the love of God. Our soul is then truly simple, when we have no aim at all but this, in all we do."

~ST. FRANCIS DE SALES

Pray

Make me single-minded, God. I know that if I focus only on loving you, all else will fall into place. Give me grace to do that.

Act

Memorize this Act of Charity: "O my God, I love you above all things with my whole heart and soul, because you are all good and worthy of all my love. I love my neighbor as myself for the love of you. I forgive all who have injured me and ask pardon of all whom I have injured. Amen." Pray it today as you clean the kitchen.

August 4

Think

"It should be observed that perfect love of God consists not in those delights, tears, and sentiments of devotion that we generally seek, but in a strong determination and keen desire to please God in all things, and to take care, as far as possible, not to offend him, and to promote his glory."

~St. Teresa of Avila

Pray

God, please inspire me to be faithful. Help me to seek you even when I don't feel all those sentiments of devotion. Strengthen my resolve to devote my heart to prayer and then my hands to your service.

Act

How is your quiet time lately? Set your alarm for fifteen minutes earlier than usual. Fix a cup of something hot to hold in your hands and keep you awake. Give God the first moments of your day and watch what he gives back to you in love.

August 5

Think

"Merit consists in the virtue of love alone, flavored with the light of true discretion, without which the soul is worth nothing."

~St. Catherine of Siena

Pray

I sometimes am guilty of performing my duties without love, Lord. I grow bitter and resentful. I let anger fester in my heart. Help me today to let go of my selfishness. Open my soul to receive your graces and teach me love as you do.

Act

When was the last time you took a family trip, even for just a day away? Plan one today.

AUGUST 6

Think

"True virtue has no limits, but goes on and on, and especially holy charity, which is the virtue of virtues, and which having a definite object, would become infinite if it could meet with a heart capable of infinity."

~St. Francis de Sales

Pray

Dear Lord, multiply the love I know in my heart. Let it grow and overflow to bless everyone in my life.

Act

Host a "crafternoon." Gather up the neighborhood kids for one last bash before school starts. Do a simple craft project together. Be sure to include cookies and ample amounts of lemonade. Share genuine, heartfelt love with the children who are your neighbors, especially those who test the limits of your virtue.

Think

"We should love and feel compassion for those who unjustly oppose us, since they harm themselves and do us good, for they adorn us with crowns of everlasting glory."

~St. Anthony Mary Zaccaria

Pray

Bless all my enemies, Lord. Draw them closer to you and prepare them for eternity with you forever in heaven.

Act

Think of a celebrity (or a politician) who takes a public stance against the Church. Post a picture of that person on your refrigerator and every time you look at it, say a Hail Mary for that person's conversion.

Think

"The proof of love is in the works. Where love exists, it works great things. But when it ceases to act, it ceases to exist."

~Pope St. Gregory the Great

Pray

Dear Lord, are there people in my life who don't know how much I love them? Teach me their love languages, and help me to meet them where they are and show them how much they are loved.

Act

Sit quietly with the above prayer for a few moments. What works would the Spirit have you do? Whom would he have you bless today? Obey without hesitation!

Think

"Do not love the world or the things of the world. If anyone loves the world, the love of the Father is not in him."

~1 John 2:15

Pray

God, show me what worldly thing is standing in the way of my growing in your love today. Give me the strength I need to remove it.

Act

If there is something you think might be an obstacle between you and God, try this experiment: Just for one day, remove that thing—whether it be shopping, working, computer time, phone conversations, or overeating—and see how God speaks to you in the spaces that open up.

Think

"I am the vine, you are the branches. Whoever remains in me and I in him will bear much fruit, because without me you can do nothing."

~John 15:5

Pray

Jesus, you tell me that I will bear much fruit if only I remain in you. I know there are places in my life where I have blocked the channels of your love. Show me those places and help me to open myself to you so that I can bring your fruit to the world in great abundance.

Act

Remember that sin cuts us off from God's grace. Without his grace, we can do nothing. It's time to go to confession. Remove the obstacles to grace and let God's love flourish in your life.

Think

"God is love, and all his operations proceed from love. Once he wills to manifest that goodness by sharing his love outside himself, then the Incarnation becomes the supreme manifestation of his goodness and love and glory."

~St. Lawrence of Brindisi

Pray

Remind me that you are love, God. I can't love my family, my friends, or even myself without first knowing and loving you.

Act

What is your favorite love song? Listen to the lyrics, replacing the word love with "God" or "Jesus," and see what message you hear.

Think

"Love consumes us only in the measure of our self-surrender."

~St. Thérèse of Lisieux

Pray

God, St. Thérèse always reminds me that you love me more than I could ever imagine. Today, remind me that, to surrender to your will, I also have to love myself. Help me to see myself as you do and to be as kind to myself as I am to my most fragile child.

Act

Turn off the negative internal conversation you are having with yourself. Be charitable towards yourself. Beg for grace and then grant yourself the benefit of knowing that you are loved by an all-knowing God. Then, extend that same grace to someone else who might be feeling as if he or she is not worthy of love.

Think

"How beautiful it is to behold a person destitute of all attachment, ready for any act of virtue or charity, gentle to all, indifferent as to any employment, serene in consolations and tribulations, and wholly content if only the will of God be done."

~St. Francis de Sales

Pray

Human love fails me sometimes, God. In my marriage, we get tired, stressed, and angry. We take one another for granted and grow thoughtless. Renew my love for my husband today. Make me wholly his and him wholly mine. Unite us in all sweetness and charity.

Act

Think of a time in your first year of marriage that you and your husband shared some special time together and felt especially close. As much as possible, recreate that time today—with food, location, clothing, or conversation.

August 14

Think

"I must anticipate the desires of others. [We should] show that we are much obliged, very honored to be able to render service. . . . The good Lord wants me to forget myself in order to give pleasure to others."

~St. Thérèse of Lisieux

Pray

You have blessed me abundantly, Lord, with people to serve. Please grant me the clarity to know their desires as well as their needs and give me the ability to sweeten their lives with acts of love.

Act

Think of each member of your immediate family. Make a list of one "want" each of them has: a little gift, some special time alone with you, a favorite meal. Write a firm plan to make each one of those things happen as soon as possible. Get to it!

Think

"A great sign appeared in the sky, a woman clothed with the sun, with the moon under her feet, and on her head a crown of twelve stars."

~REVELATION 12:1

Pray

Mary, on this Feast of the Assumption, when we remember your assumption into heaven, grant me the grace I need to follow you there. Hold me close; help me to be the wife, mother, and daughter of God I am meant to be.

Act

Before Mass today, pick some flowers (or buy some). At church, leave them at Our Lady's feet and ask her to watch over your family and bless your motherhood.

Think

"By our little acts of charity practiced in the shade we convert souls far away, we help missionaries, we win for them abundant alms; and by that means build actual dwellings spiritual and material for our Eucharistic Lord."

~St. Thérèse of Lisieux

Pray

Sometimes, in the comfort of my own home, I forget about missionaries—those brave souls far away, who overcome so many obstacles to bring the Good News to all your people. Bless them, Lord! Show me how you would have me participate in their work so that I, too, can make believers of all nations.

Act

Make a missionary prayer board. Decorate the plain frame of a large cork bulletin board with ribbons and buttons or whatever you have on hand. Print pictures and stories of missions around the world that will remind you to pray for the intentions of the missionaries every day. Check these sites for missionary organizations: catholicworldmission.org, pallotticenter. org, and glenmary.org.

Think

"The Lord measures our perfection not by the number and greatness of the works we do for him, but by our manner of doing them. And this manner is only the love of God with which, and for which, we do them. They are more perfect as they are done with more pure and perfect love, and as they are less mingled with the thoughts of pleasure or praise in this life or the other."

~St. John of the Cross

Pray

I want to do all things in love, Lord. Take my humble gifts and my meager affections and wash them with your love. Make me a gift of grace to all who cross my path today.

Act

Love means listening. Spend some time alone with your quietest child today. Ask questions and truly listen to the answers. Enter your child's world and do your best to see his or her perspective.

Think

"The real strength of love consists not in enjoying the divine sweetness, but rather in exact observance of the Rules, and the faithful practice of solid virtue—that is, in humility, the love of self-contempt, patient endurance of insults and adversities, self-forgetfulness, and a love that seeks not to be known except by God. This alone is true love, and these are its unerring tokens. May God preserve us from that sensible love which allows us to live in ourselves, while the true leads us to die to ourselves."

~St. Jane Frances de Chantal

Pray

God, ignite in me a fire of humility which will consume all self-serving, prideful inclinations. Remind me again and again that I am nothing without you and that I can do all things in you.

Act

St. Jane Frances de Chantal is the patroness of in-law problems. Even if you have no problems with your in-laws, go out of your way to express your love to them today.

August 19

Think

"Do not lose such an excellent time for talking with [Jesus] as the hour after Communion. Remember that this is a very profitable hour for the soul; if you spend it in the company of the good Jesus, you are doing him a great service. . . . Kiss his feet in gratitude."

~Bl. Teresa of Avila

Pray

Bring me closer to you through the Eucharist, Lord. Feed me, fill me, and make me whole.

Act

Go to Mass today and offer your Communion for those who don't know Christ in the Eucharist. If you can't get to church, pray this spiritual communion at home: "My Jesus, I believe that you are present in the Most Holy Sacrament. I love you above all things, and I desire to receive you into my soul. Since I cannot at this moment receive you sacramentally, come at least spiritually into my heart. I embrace you as if you were already there and unite myself wholly to you. Never permit me to be separated from you. Amen."

Think

"Be kind and merciful. Let no one ever come to you without coming away better and happier. Be the living expression of God's kindness."

~Bl. Teresa of Calcutta

Pray

Today, sweet Jesus, let me live this quote intentionally. In everyone I meet, grant me the grace to see an opportunity to make their lives better and happier.

Act

If you find yourself in a grocery store or big box store today, look for a mother who is trying valiantly to juggle shopping and small children. Give her a smile, a word of encouragement, and some kind of tangible help. Make it your personal apostolate to make the life of young mothers a little brighter every time you shop, even if you are one of those young mothers yourself.

Think

"To love God as he ought to be loved, we must be detached from all temporal love. We must love nothing but him, or if we love anything else, we must love it only for his sake."

~St. Peter Claver

Pray

Dear God, remind me that you must always come first—not because you are selfish or greedy, but because you are the source of all love. Without that love, we are nothing.

Act

Put God first in all the little details of your routine today. Before you begin any new task, give it first to God. For example, "I love you, Lord. I fold this laundry for love of you."

Think

"The surest way to discover whether we have the love of God is to see whether we love our neighbor, for the two things are never separated. Be sure, too, that the more you perceive yourself to advance in the love of your neighbor, the more you will do so in that of God. To see how much we love our neighbor is the surest rule by which to find out how much we love God."

~St. Teresa of Avila

Pray

God, I love you! Increase in me a genuine love for neighbor. Let me see you in the man next door, the woman waiting for my parking space, the correspondent online, the person on the other end of the phone. And grant that they find you in me.

Act

Bring your neighbors' trash can up from the curb on garbage day or leave an unexpected baked treat or bouquet of flowers on their doorstep.

Think

"Alas! We have not as much love as we need! I mean that it would require an infinite amount to have enough to love our God according to his due; and yet, miserable that we are, we throw it away lavishly upon vile and unworthy objects, as if we had a superfluity."

~St. Francis de Sales

Pray

Dear God, the world can be such a tempting and distracting place. How you must sigh when I set you aside again and again in pursuit of fleeting pleasures. Show me where I "throw away" my love today, God, and give me grace to give you all of my affection.

Act

Do you make time for pleasures and distractions but fail to make time for God? Today, set aside fifteen minutes more for prayer, alone or with your family. Ask yourself honestly if you could not make that a habit.

Think

"We should love the poor with peculiar affection, beholding in them the very person of Christ, and showing them the same consideration that he did."

~St. Vincent de Paul

Pray

Give me a heart for the poor, Lord! Though I am occupied with the needs of my own family, let me be sensitive to the needs and even the wants of others.

Act

Visit a meal delivery service. Donate flowers to be delivered with the meals and brighten someone's day with an unexpected token of beauty and dignity.

Think

"What is easier, sweeter, more pleasant, than to love goodness, beauty, and love, the fullness of which you are, O Lord, my God?"

~ST. ROBERT BELLARMINE

Pray

Dear God, help me to see you as you truly are. Fill my eyes with your irresistible beauty, glory, and love. Awaken in my heart a deeper longing to be united with you.

Act

Go outside today and look at something vast—the sky, a lake, a field, the ocean, or a mountain. Drink in the richness of God's wonders; he who hung the stars in the sky has also counted the hairs on your head.

Think

"Where there is charity and wisdom, there is neither fear nor ignorance."

~St. Francis of Assisi

Pray

As I sit with newspaper, book, or Internet today, God, help me to remember that knowledge is not an end-goal. Give me the time and the discipline to spend more time seeking wisdom and your love than I do satisfying my idle curiosity.

Act

Make a phone call today to reconnect with a family member you've been neglecting.

Think

"Love requires that we say that we love and that we repeat it in all its forms and that we praise what we love endlessly, without measure."

~Bl. Charles of Jesus

Pray

Dear God, sometimes I feel awkward talking about my faith, especially with people who don't share it. Give me grace to speak about my love for you to all people. I want to always bear witness to your goodness and glory.

Act

Tell every member of your family that you love them today in three different ways: (1) Say the words "I love you" to each of them individually. (2) Touch them. Give each of them a hug, a kiss, a pat—some physical expression of your affection. (3) Serve them. Do something small but special for each person to let them know that you notice them and that they are loved.

Think

"The measure of charity may be taken from the want of desires. As desires diminish in a soul, charity increases in it; and when it no longer feels any desire, then it possesses perfect charity."

~St. Augustine

Pray

God, make me ever more aware of the blessings of my life. Create in me a heart for sharing them with others. Crowd out any feeling of desire with intense gratitude for your great gifts.

Act

Today is the Feast of St. Augustine, the patron saint of brewers. Make beer-roasted chicken tonight. Invite your favorite priest for dinner.

Think

"Calling to mind your work of faith and labor of love and endurance in hope of our Lord Jesus Christ, before our God and Father."

~1 Thessalonians 1:3

Pray

Jesus, you are the foundation of all I do. Help me be your hands and heart, to continue to serve your people and your Church on earth.

Act

Remember that you and your family belong to a larger family—that of the Church. Write a note to your pastor thanking him for his service to God and the Church.

Think

"Accustom yourself continually to make many acts of love, for they enkindle and melt the soul."

~St. Teresa of Avila

Pray

Blessed Mother, infuse me with your sweetness! Let me never miss an opportunity to make an act of love.

Act

Say something nice to everyone you meet today. Everyone.

Think

"As for what concerns our relations with our fellow men, the anguish in our neighbor's soul must break all precept. All that we do is a means to an end, but love is an end in itself, because God is love."

~ST. EDITH STEIN

Pray

Dear God, open my heart and my eyes to see some member of your Church who needs your love. Show me how I can bring Christ and be Christ to that person in need.

Act

Think of someone in your parish or your community who might be in need—a mom with a newborn, a family in mourning, or a friend with health issues. Reach out to that person today and be attentive to their needs. Be specific: "Can I bring you a meal?" "Can I babysit?" "Can I make phone calls for you?"

SEPTEMBER

Diligence

Think

"The slack hand impoverishes, but the hand of the diligent enriches."

~PROVERBS 10:4

Pray

God, give me strength where I am weak. Help me do all things with a spirit of service to you, my family, and my community today.

Act

Spend some time today organizing your calendar for the month. Whatever system you use, make it neat and clean—easy for you and your family to consult and follow.

Think

"First, upon awakening in the morning, turn your thoughts to God present everywhere; place your heart and your entire being in his hands. Then think briefly of the good you will be able to accomplish that day and the evil you can avoid, especially by controlling your predominant fault."

~St. Jane Frances de Chantal

Pray

God, please show me the good you would have me do. I beg you to reveal to me my predominant fault. Let me see it as you see it. Then, grant me the grace to control the fault and to do your will.

Act

Follow St. Jane Frances de Chantal's direction exactly, before you do anything else today: Turn your thoughts to God and place yourself in his hands. Think of the good you can accomplish. Think of your predominant fault. Resolve to do good and to avoid that fault. Ask for the diligence to keep your resolution. Kneel down, adore God, and thank him for all the grace he has given you.

September 3

Think

"Therefore, my beloved brethren, be firm, steadfast, always fully devoted to the work of the Lord, knowing that in the Lord your labor is not in vain."

~1 Corinthians 15:58

Pray

Dear Jesus, all the work I must do in a day can sometimes be exhausting and distracting. When I am frazzled, help me remember heavenly goals for myself and my family. Keep me focused on the work that really matters.

Act

Is there a household task you keep for yourself because it's too much bother to teach a child to "help" you? Do that task with a child today. Let go of perfection and smile your way through it.

Think

"An old habit is not easily broken, and no man will readily be moved from his own will; but if you cling more to your own will or to your own reason than to the humble obedience of Jesus Christ, it will be long before you are a man illumined by grace. Almighty God wills that we be perfectly subject and obedient to him, and that we rise high above our own will and our own reason by a great burning love and a complete desire for him."

~Thomas à Kempis

Pray

God, show every member of our family the habit you want us to break. Then grant us the grace to work diligently to replace it with a virtue.

Act

With your family, make a list of one habit each that you will break this month. For each bad habit, decide upon a virtue with which to replace it. Post the list of each person's virtue goals. Pray for each other's progress towards those virtues every day in September.

September 5

Think

"First tell the devil to rest, and then I'll rest too."

~St. John Bosco

Pray

God, sometimes I think my family only notices the housework when it doesn't get done. Help me to remember that even if no one else sees, you see my efforts and will reward them accordingly.

Act

Set a timer and spend fifteen minutes performing some small, unnoticed housekeeping task in your home—organize a sock drawer, neaten a bookcase, or wipe the baseboards. You choose. And you do it.

September 6

Think

"There is always the danger that we may just do the work for the sake of the work. This is where the respect and the love and the devotion come in—that we do it to God, to Christ, and that's why we try to do it as beautifully as possible."

~Bl. Teresa of Calcutta

Pray

God, let me remember that every task I do, I do for you and that you are love. Infuse me with your love and let me bring that love to my family through my work.

Act

Nothing is more beautiful to a child than his mother's smile. With every task, at every chore, be sure to smile. And every time you address a child's needs, do it with a warm and genuine smile.

Think

"Unless the Lord build the house, they labor in vain who build. Unless the Lord guard the city, in vain does the guard keep watch."

~PSALM 127:1

Pray

God, help me to see my life with your eyes. Point out to me my flaws and give me grace to improve them.

Act

Take a trash bag into the most cluttered room of your house and fill it with at least ten items. Tie the bag and throw it away. Don't think about it again.

Think

"I grieve for you, O Mary most sorrowful, for the pangs that wrenched your most loving heart at the burial of Jesus. Dear Mother, by your heart sunk in the bitterness of desolation, obtain for me the virtue of diligence and the gift of wisdom."

~The Seven Dolors of the Blessed Virgin Mary

Pray

Blessed Mother, from the moment you were conceived, God knew the sorrow you would experience. He knew the joy you'd bring to the life of the Divine Infant too. Today, as we celebrate your birthday, help us to remember that even in your sorrows, you were faithful and obedient. You are for us the perfect model of joyful diligence.

Act

Bake cupcakes for the Blessed Mother today and frost them blue. Talk with your family about all the ways Mary was diligent and wise.

Think

"I am not sure exactly what heaven will be like, but I do know that when we die and it comes time for God to judge us, he will not ask, "How many good things have you done in your life?" Rather he will ask, "How much love did you put into what you did?""

~BL. TERESA OF CALCUTTA

Pray

God, when I am tempted to complain, remind me of your patient love. Help me to emulate that kind of self-giving in all that I do.

Act

Clean your oven or your refrigerator today. Whichever one needs it most. Do a thorough job without complaint.

Think

"The goal of all our undertakings should be not so much a task perfectly completed as the accomplishment of the will of God."

~St. Thérèse of Lisieux

Pray

Merciful Jesus, help me to let go of the tight grip I hold on perfectionism. Put my hand instead into yours, and help me know your will.

Act

Do one thing today that you are quite sure you cannot do perfectly. Instead, do it cheerfully.

Think

"All devotion which leads to sloth is false. We must love work."

~St. Zita

Pray

Dear Jesus, when I am tempted to think a job is "too dull" or "too menial" for me to perform, remind me of the menial tasks you performed in your hidden life in Nazareth. Inspire me to follow your example and serve God by serving others.

Act

Where do you cut corners? Meal planning? House-keeping? Prayer life? Pick your weakest link today and spend some time improving your efforts.

Think

"Well, come now, my daughters, don't be sad when obedience draws you to involvement in exterior matters. Know that if it is in the kitchen, the Lord walks among the pots and pans, helping you both interiorly and exteriorly."

~St. Teresa of Avila

Pray

Dear sweet Lord, help me to see you here in my kitchen. Let me see you in the faces of the children who interrupt me when I cook and clean. Let me see you in the face of my husband as he eats the meal I prepare. Let me be grateful for the work I have to do amidst the pots and pans today.

Act

Bring love out of your kitchen today. Cook a nice meal, perhaps with a special dessert, and pay special attention to cleaning the kitchen well. Pray for your family as you work.

Think

"When we once begin to form good resolutions, God gives us every opportunity of carrying them out."

~St. John Chrysostom

Pray

God, it can be so hard to be interrupted! Give me grace to remember that my children and my family's needs are not distractions from my work. They are my work.

Act

Clean your bathroom today. Not a "surface" cleaning, but a real cleaning—all the way to the corners, even the places no one will notice.

Think

"I have seen through experience the great good that comes to a soul when it does not turn aside from obedience. It is through this practice that I think one advances in virtue and gains humility."

~St. Teresa of Avila

Pray

God, grant me the patience that I need to advance in virtue. Grant me the clarity of vision that I need to remember always that I am nothing without you, and I cannot work without your grace. Grant that same grace to my children, that they may grow in virtue.

Act

Today, require obedience of your children every single time you ask for it. Do not be harsh. Be cheerful. Be patient. Be diligent.

Think

"Prayer is powerful beyond limits when we turn to the Immaculata, who is queen even of God's heart."

~St. Maximilian Kolbe

Pray

Holy Mary, on this Feast of Our Lady of Sorrows, imprint upon my heart the sufferings of Christ and teach me to accept suffering as you did—for the love of God, in reparation for sin, for the conversion of sinners.

Act

Embrace all of your suffering today before it happens. See each small sacrifice as a gift from God—one that you can give back to him with love. Kiss your crosses.

Think

"In fact, when we were with you, we instructed you that if anyone was unwilling to work, neither should that one eat."

~2 Thessalonians 3:10

Pray

Dear Lord, thank you for the work you allow us to do, and thank you for providing so abundantly for our needs. Make us ever grateful to you for our ability to work.

Act

If you have not memorized the above quote from scripture, memorize it with your family today. It will serve you well for many years.

Think

"Sweet Lord, you are meek and merciful. Who would not give himself wholeheartedly to your service, if he began to taste even a little of your fatherly rule?"

~St. Robert Bellarmine

Pray

Dear God, thank you for the gifts of wisdom and intelligence you gave your humble servant, St. Bellarmine. He used these gifts for good, to defend your Church on earth. As I reflect on St. Bellarmine's feast day, help me too to use the gifts of my mind and body to serve you always.

Act

Have your children copy their favorite scripture passage in their best handwriting. Give the same "assignment" to yourself. Post them together on the refrigerator for the family to read and remember today.

Think

"One cannot desire freedom from the Cross when one is especially chosen for the Cross."

~St. Edith Stein

Pray

St. Edith Stein, please pray for me. Ask God to show me the crosses in the lives of the people I love, and ask him for the strength and grace to help carry those crosses. I want to be a blessing to the dear ones he has given to me.

Act

Do you have a child who is not particularly diligent about cleaning his room? Do it for him today. Surprise him. Establish order in his room cheerfully and skillfully. Leave him a note letting him know how glad you were to be able to give him the gift of a fresh start.

SEPTEMBER 19

Think

"Without work, it is impossible to have fun."

~St. Thomas Aquinas

Pray

Lord, keep me focused on the corporal works of mercy today. Help me to see how my daily work feeds the hungry, clothes the naked, and gives drink to the thirsty.

Act

Is there some special meal your family enjoys but you have been avoiding because of the work involved in preparing it? Plan that meal for tonight.

Think

"The way Jesus shows you is not easy. Rather, it is like a path winding up a mountain. Do not lose heart! The steeper the road, the faster it rises towards ever wider horizons."

~Bl. John Paul II

Pray

God, don't let me climb this mountain looking down. Instead, lift my chin. Whisper to me to open my eyes and look toward that wide horizon. Push me toward it, Lord—toward the wide, wonderful world you created for me.

Act

Put on some happy music today—something that will encourage you to sing along or whistle while you work. Then, tackle the chore that looks like the steepest climb. You can do it! Get it done and then remember to stop and enjoy the view.

Think

"Let us love God, but with the strength of our arms, in the sweat of our brow."

~St. Vincent de Paul

Pray

God, help me find balance between work and leisure activities. Show me ways to use to the gift of time to better serve you.

Act

Spend some time today looking at the structure of your days. Look for ways you routinely waste time (television? phone? computer?). Plan more constructive tasks to replace at least some of these activities.

Think

"How long, O sluggard, will you rest? When will you rise from your sleep? A little sleep, a little slumber, a little folding of the arms to rest—then will poverty come upon you like a highway man, and want like an armed man."

~PROVERBS 6:9-11

Pray

God, thank you for the gift of sleep, for allowing my mind and my body to rest in you. Thank you for the gift of this new day and for the time that stretches before me. When I am at work, let me work with all diligence for your glory. When I am at rest, let my soul be at peace. When rest gives way to awakening, let me embrace that heroic moment and rise to meet the new day with resolve to live for you.

Act

Set your alarm to awaken an hour earlier tomorrow. With that time, be industrious. Do that task you've been delaying. Finish it early—first thing—today.

Think

"In all the events of life, you must recognize the divine will. Adore and bless it, especially in the things which are the hardest for you."

~St. Padre Pio

Pray

Lord, I give you all of me today—especially the parts where I am weak and tempted to give up. Help me to see these weaknesses not as failures but as opportunities to grow in grace.

Act

Tonight, don't rush through bedtime routines. Give baths, read books, say prayers, sing, and snuggle. If your children are older, spend time praying with them and talking about their day.

Think

"The great danger for family life, in the midst of any society whose idols are pleasure, comfort, and independence, lies in the fact that people close their hearts and become selfish."

~Bl. John Paul II

Pray

Dear God, make me keenly aware of the needs of others today. Use me as your instrument to meet those needs.

Act

The first time you want to take some "me" time today, turn your attention instead to the neediest member of your family. Open your heart wide to his needs and pour yourself into meeting them.

Think

"Faithful obedience would have wrought more in the sight of God and in the hearts of men than all your human prudence."

~St. Catherine of Siena

Pray

God, help me to hear your voice in the voices of my children and husband today. Show me the ways that I can better serve you by finding out their needs and meeting them.

Act

What is something you can do today to make your house a more pleasant place to be? You might clear the walkway of debris, bake a treat, or declutter the family room. Whatever you choose, do that job today—not for appreciation, but as an act of love and service.

Think

"Since we know the path by which we must please God, which is that of the commandments and counsels, we should follow it very diligently, and think of his life and death and of the many things we owe him; let the rest come when the Lord desires."

~ St. Teresa of Avila

Pray

Jesus, when I focus on your life and your death, it is so easy for me to see the path you've made for me. Help me to keep my focus sharp.

Act

Read the Beatitudes today (Matthew 5:3). God's message is crystal clear. Make a firm resolution to follow the path he has lit for you.

Think

"We should assist the poor in every way, and do it both by ourselves and by enlisting the help of others. Give me persons of prayer and they will be capable of anything."

~St. Vincent de Paul

Pray

Dear God, St. Vincent was known especially for his love and service to the poor. Help me to see beyond my own needs and wants so that I might be of service to those around me—family, friends, coworkers, and even strangers I might meet today.

Act

Think of someone you know who could use your help and attention. An exhausted new mom? A lonely neighbor? Drop by with muffins or make a phone call and ask how you can help. Listen.

Think

"You will hear at the end those sweet words: 'Come my blessed son, and possess the kingdom of heaven, because you conscientiously cast aside desire and affection for conformity to the world, and reared and nurtured your family in holy fear of me. Now I am giving you perfect rest.'"

~St. Catherine of Siena

Pray

The world calls so loudly for my attention, God. Its noise often distracts me from the work you would have me do. Give me the wisdom to discern your voice above the din and the strength to cast aside my wayward desires.

Act

Turn off the noise of the world today. Don't listen to the radio or television. Be still and quiet. Focus on what God would have you do to rear and nurture your family for him.

Think

"Bless the Lord, all you angels, mighty in strength and attentive, obedient to every command."

~PSALM 103:20

Pray

All angels in heaven, be my strength, my light, and my support as I seek to do God's will here on earth. Help me fight weakness and temptation. Make me a great warrior for Christ in all I do.

Act

Ask God to show you a place where you have let weakness or sloth become a habit in your life. Rip it out and replace it with work and prayer.

Think

"You know that our Lord does not look at the greatness or difficulty of our action, but at the love with which you do it. What, then, have you to fear?"

~St. Thérèse of Lisieux

Pray

St. Thérèse, you died on this day in 1897 and your great desire was to intercede in heaven for those of us on earth. Ask the Child Jesus today to grant me all the graces I need to be diligent to do for God the work that he ordains for me. Like you, I want nothing more than to do every small thing he asks with great love.

Act

Look around carefully today. Look and ask yourself what are the small things that matter to God. Do them with great love.

OCTOBER

Patience

OCTOBER 1

Think

"If I did not simply suffer from one moment to another, it would be impossible for me to be patient; but I look only at the present moment. I forget the past and I take good care not to forestall the future. When we yield to discouragement or despair it is usually because we give too much thought to the past and to the future."

~ST. THÉRÈSE OF LISIEUX

Pray

Just for today, God, give me the grace to live in the moment. Let me not lament the past or worry about the future. Let me rest patiently in your love today.

Act

After asking St. Thérèse for whom, buy a rose or roses for someone. Bless that person with a shower of roses in honor of the Little Flower, whose feast is today.

Think

"God does not ask of us the perfection of tomorrow, nor even of tonight, but only of the present moment."

~St. Dominic Savio

Pray

God, help me to live in the moment today. I want to say "yes" to you today, minute by minute, one task at a time.

Act

Don't wear your watch today. Every time you catch yourself attempting to check the time, say a prayer instead, asking God for patience.

Think

"Patience is the companion of wisdom."

~St. Augustine

Pray

God, I try so hard sometimes to be wise. Let me see instead that I must be patient. Wisdom and patience are good friends. One attracts the other.

Act

Listen to a child today. Don't say any more than necessary to get her talking and keep her talking. Be patient with the rambling stories, and see how much a child can teach you.

Think

"Be faithful in small things because it is in them that your strength lies."

~Bl. Teresa of Calcutta

Pray

God, I know that I can please you with my faithfulness in small things, but it can be so frustrating sometimes to never see the "big picture." Today, help to keep me focused on my heavenly goals—and all the small steps I must take to get there.

Act

Children and the elderly have many things in common, including a capacity for slow and deliberate attention to small things. Bring your children to visit an older person you know today. Sit, talk, and just be with them.

OCTOBER 5

Think

"Have patience with all things, but chiefly have patience with yourself. Do not lose courage in considering your own imperfections but instantly set about remedying them—every day begin the task anew."

~ST. FRANCIS DE SALES

Pray

I want to see myself as you see me God. Grant me the grace to remedy my imperfections and to make myself the person you intend me to be. Help me to be kind and patient with myself in the process.

Act

Speak kindly to yourself today. Turn off all negative internal dialogue and only say things to yourself that you would say to your dearest friend.

Think

"The prayer of the sick person is his patience and his acceptance of his sickness for the love of Jesus Christ. Make sickness itself a prayer, for there is none more powerful, save martyrdom!"

~St. Francis de Sales

Pray

Lord, even when my body is healthy, my soul is weak and flawed. Help me to accept my limitations, both physical and spiritual. Remind me that, when I offer them to you, my frustrations can become a source of grace and the beginning of good health.

Act

Make a small change to take better care of yourself today. Without worrying about seeing "results," eat your vegetables, drink water, and make time for exercise. Focus on these small steps.

Think

"If there be a true way that leads to the Everlasting Kingdom, it is most certainly that of suffering, patiently endured."

~St. Colette

Pray

Dear Jesus, every Christian suffers. You've chosen the perfect cross for each one of us. Please help me to recognize my cross and to bear it patiently.

Act

Do you know someone who is suffering right now? What can you do to help her carry her cross? Do it today.

October 8

Think

"Can we then do more wisely than refer everything to God's care? Can our future be in greater safety than in the almighty hands of that adorable Master, that good and tender Father who loves us much more than we love ourselves? Where shall we find a safer refuge than in the maternal bosom of his loving Providence?"

~Fr. Jean-Pierre de Caussade

Pray

When I am tired and hurting, Lord, I am often tempted to lash out in anger. Help me to recall your patient endurance of the cross and renew my resolve to endure all with patience for you.

Act

What bothers you? Is there some silly thing that makes you want to scream? Write it down on a small piece of paper and tuck it behind a crucifix somewhere in your home. When that thing happens, remember that you have already given the annoyance of it over to Jesus and . . . smile.

OCTOBER 9

Think

"So you've been hauled over the coals? Don't follow the advice of pride and lose your temper. Think: 'How charitable they are toward me! The things they've left unsaid!'"

~St. Josemaria Escriva

Pray

Sweet Jesus, I talk too much. I sigh too often. Please give me sufficient grace to keep my mouth closed in the face of trials.

Act

What is it that you are avoiding? Do that thing today and suffer through it with a silent smile.

October 10

Think

"Therefore, be constant in practicing every virtue, and especially in imitating the patience of our dear Jesus, for this is the summit of pure love. Live in such a way that all may know that you bear outwardly as well as inwardly the image of Christ crucified, the model of all gentleness and mercy."

~St. Paul of the Cross

Pray

You did not only accept your cross, Jesus, you embraced it. Help me to embrace every cross that comes my way today.

Act

Is there someone you avoid because he or she talks too much? Call that person today, open your heart, and listen.

OCTOBER 11

Think

"Let nothing trouble you. Let nothing make you afraid. All things pass away. God never changes. Patience obtains everything. God alone is enough."

~St. Teresa of Avila

Pray

Jesus, you are the perfect example of patient endurance. Help me to remember that you are the same God when I am facing a grave trial as when my life sparkles with joy.

Act

Copy St. Teresa of Avila's quote above and post it where you brush your teeth. Read it at least twice a day, and learn to repeat to yourself, "God is enough." Because he is.

OCTOBER 12

❀

Think

"Do not let any occasion of gaining merit pass without taking care to draw some spiritual profit from it; as, for example, from a sharp word which someone may say to you; from an act of obedience imposed against your will; from an opportunity which may occur to humble yourself, or to practice charity, sweetness, and patience."

~St. Ignatius Loyola

Pray

God, I can be so stubborn, selfish, and righteous sometimes! Give me grace to think less about myself and my desires and more about you and your desires today.

Act

Bake something with your children. Resist the urge to take over and "do it right" for them. Let them pour and mix and stir without interference. Enjoy the process without worrying about the results.

OCTOBER 13

Think

"Indeed, religion with contentment is a great gain. For we brought nothing into the world, just as we shall not be able to take anything out of it. If we have food and clothing, we shall be content with that. Those who want to be rich are falling into temptation and into a trap and into many foolish and harmful desires, which plunge them into ruin and destruction. . . . But you, man of God, avoid all this. Instead, pursue righteousness, devotion, faith, love, patience, and gentleness."

~1 TIMOTHY 6:6–11

Pray

Today, Lord, I empty myself of greed and I beg you to fill me with righteousness, godliness, faith, love, patience, and meekness.

Act

This is a glorious time of year! No matter where you live, God's abundant riches are evident in nature. Get outside and breathe deeply of the blessings of autumn. Go someplace beautiful and count the blessings around you.

Think

"If you seek patience, you will find no better example than the cross. Great patience occurs in two ways: either when one patiently suffers much, or when one suffers things which one is able to avoid and yet does not avoid. Christ endured much on the cross, and did so patiently, because when he suffered he did not threaten; he was led like a sheep to the slaughter and he did not open his mouth."

~ St. Thomas Aquinas

Pray

Good Shepherd, I want to follow you. Keep my eyes focused on your face and my ears tuned to your voice.

Act

Set a timer to go off once an hour today. Every time it rings, turn your heart toward God and offer him the next sixty minutes of your day.

October 15

Think

"I complained to him for consenting that I should suffer so many torments. But this suffering was well repaid, for almost always the favors afterward came in great abundance. I only think that the soul comes out of the crucible like gold, more refined and purified, so as to see the Lord within itself."

~St. Teresa of Avila

Pray

I need you, God. I need you to help me to see that my suffering is a favor. If I just conform my will to yours, my soul will be refined.

Act

Don't complain today. Instead, find opportunities to praise others—praise your husband, your children, and your Creator.

OCTOBER 16

Think

"Let us stand fast in what is right, and prepare our souls for trial. Let us wait upon God's strengthening aid and say to him: 'O Lord, you have been our refuge in all generations.'"

~St. Boniface

Pray

Give me courage, Lord, always to speak the truth and stand up for what is right, even when all seems lost and the cause feels hopeless. Help me to see the value in remaining steadfast, even in the face of defeat.

Act

Make a small change toward justice today. Wear a "precious feet" pin to show support for pro-life causes. Put a bumper sticker on your car. Write a letter to the editor of your local paper.

Think

"Have patience; and do not let your minds and hearts be filled with evil thoughts and fancies which come from the devil to impede the honor of God and the salvation of souls and your own peace and quiet."

~St. Catherine of Siena

Pray

Let me take every thought captive. Jesus, box up those thoughts that are not of God. Bring to my soul a sense of peace and quiet.

Act

No matter what you have to do to make it happen, spend fifteen minutes today in peace and quiet, with your heart and mind fixed steadily on God alone.

October 18

Think

"Are you making no progress in prayer? Then you need only offer God the prayers which the Savior has poured out for us in the sacrament of the altar. Offer God his fervent love in reparation for your sluggishness."

~St. Margaret Mary Alacoque

Pray

God, help me to remember that my spiritual life is not about me; it's about you. Show me how to give all of me to you—even my failings and frustrations.

Act

Make time for ten minutes of quiet today. No mental grocery list-making! Do nothing for those ten minutes but sit in God's presence and open your heart to hear his voice.

October 19

Think

"But truly, you cannot at first arrive at such consolations without struggle and labor that must precede. Your old habits will somewhat forestall you, but better habits can overcome the old ones."

~Thomas à Kempis

Pray

God, help me to accept that life is not without struggle. Give me grace to embrace the struggle and understand that the journey will strengthen me as I recognize and abandon my bad habits, replacing them with good ones.

Act

Tackle a big outdoor job today. Rake leaves or ready the garden for winter. As you work, be mindful that there is joy in the journey; there is beauty awaiting you in the muck.

Think

"And when night comes, and you look back over the day and see how fragmentary everything has been, and how much you planned that has gone undone, and all the reasons you have to be embarrassed and ashamed: just take everything exactly as it is, put it in God's hands and leave it with Him."

~St. Edith Stein

Pray

Jesus, you fell three times while carrying the cross. Help me see my weaknesses as a call to lean on your strength and grow ever closer to you.

Act

Before you go to bed tonight, write down all of the things you did wrong or failed to accomplish in your day. Pray over your list, asking God to complete you where you fall short. Then crumple up the paper, throw it away, and get a good night's sleep before tackling a new day.

Think

"The truly patient man and true servant of God bears up equally under tribulations accompanied by ignominy and those that bring honor. To be despised, criticized, or accused by evil men is a slight thing to a courageous man, but to be criticized, denounced, and treated badly by good men, by our own friends and relations is a test of virtue."

~St. Francis de Sales

Pray

Dear Lord, as I call to mind the friends who have hurt me, I forgive them with a sincere heart and I sincerely promise you (and myself) to never revisit that injury.

Act

Deliberately speak well today of someone who has spoken ill of you in the past.

Think

"A nation of firm purpose you keep in peace; in peace, for its trust in you."

~Isaiah 26:3

Pray

When I grow anxious with impatience, Lord, remind me of the serenity that is found in turning my thoughts to you. Our time is not your time. Give me more of your perspective on eternity.

Act

Spend some time looking through old family photos today. Remember that today you are making tomorrow's memories.

OCTOBER 23

Think

"I . . . challenge you to a sweet and most holy patience, for without patience we cannot please God. I beg you then to take up this weaponry of patience so that you may receive the fruit of your troubles."

~St. Catherine of Siena

Pray

Infuse my soul with sweet patience, Lord. Make my heart like yours.

Act

Make something sweet for your family tonight. Invite your most challenging child to help you in the kitchen. Be as sweet as what you're making.

Think

"Love is patient, love is kind. It is not jealous, (love) is not pompous, it is not inflated, it is not rude, it does not seek its own interests, it is not quick-tempered, it does not brood over injury, it does not rejoice over wrongdoing but rejoices with the truth. It bears all things, believes all things, hopes all things, endures all things."

~1 CORINTHIANS 13:4–7

Pray

Thank you, Lord, for the gift of my husband who has endured these years with me. Help me bring him closer to heaven today.

Act

When things get tense sometime today, stop yourself before reacting. Breathe in, breathe out. Breathe in, breathe out. Repeat as many times as necessary until the urge to overreact passes.

OCTOBER 25

Think

"Amid the difficulties you meet in the exercise of devotion, remember the words of our Lord: 'A woman about to give birth has great sorrow, but when she has brought forth her child, she no longer remembers the anguish for joy that a man is born into the world.' Within your soul you have Jesus Christ, the most precious child in the world, and until he is entirely brought forth and born, you cannot help suffering from your labor."

~St. Francis de Sales

Pray

These are days, God, of much labor and fatigue. My life is full and my family needs so much from me. Let me remember in the pains of my labor that my goal is to bring you forth in my soul.

Act

Do chores alongside your children today. Make cheerful conversation with them while you work. Listen to what they tell you.

OCTOBER 26

Think

"The patient and humble endurance of the cross, whatever nature it may be, is the highest work we have to do."
~St. Katherine Drexel

Pray

Your yoke is easy and your burden is light, Lord. I am sorry for the times I have sought to throw off the burdens you would have me carry.

Act

You are suffering many things, but others are too. Call someone you know who is struggling. Offer to pray for and with her. Listen to her thoughts, complaints, and worries, and resist the urge to share any of your own.

OCTOBER 27

Think

"Be patient and leave it in the hands of God. . . . In every event the best we can do is leave ourselves in the hands of God."

~St. Teresa of Avila

Pray

I am entirely in your hands, God. Show me how you would have me spend my time, what you would have me say, and where you would have me go.

Act

Spend some time in front of the Blessed Sacrament today. Pray for patience.

Think

"When you feel the assaults of passion and anger, then is the time to be silent as Jesus was silent in the midst of His ignominies and sufferings."

~ST. PAUL OF THE CROSS

Pray

I am so restless, Jesus. Enter my heart, suppress my anxious thoughts, and make me still.

Act

When you make a to-do list today, write a separate list alongside your daily tasks. Write out a "big picture to-do list" including items, such as "instill a love for God in the hearts of my children" and "obtain heaven for myself and my family." Let these give you perspective in your work today.

Think

"Life is a journey, not a destination."

~St. Thérèse of Lisieux

Pray

St. Thérèse, please pray that I will be mindful of the joy in the journey and that I will never take my eyes off my ultimate destination of heaven.

Act

Take a walk with your family after dinner tonight. Emphasize the joy of just walking together. Surprise them with dessert when you return home. There can be joy in the journey and the destination.

Think

"Never be in a hurry; do everything quietly and in a calm spirit. Do not lose your inner peace for anything whatsoever, even if your whole world seems upset."

~St. Francis de Sales

Pray

When I rush, I forget you, Lord. As many times as you need to today, push my "pause button." Slow my steps and turn my heart toward you.

Act

Any time a child seeks your attention today, stop what you are doing and give it. Turn off the computer, hang up the phone, put down the dish towel, and listen. Through that small voice, God is speaking to you.

Think

"Don't force yourself to pray, for a simple adherence to God's will, expressed from time to time, is enough. Moreover, suffering borne in the will quietly and patiently is a continual, very powerful prayer before God, regardless of the complaints and anxieties that come from the inferior part of the soul."

~St. Jane Frances de Chantal

Pray

Every life has some pain, Lord, and mine is no exception. Help me to bear my pains quietly and patiently.

Act

Pray for someone who is in pain today. Help her to carry her cross. Better yet, bake a batch of muffins and bring them to her. Share a quiet cup of tea and offer to pray with her.

NOVEMBER

Gratitude

Think

"For me, prayer means launching out of the heart toward God; a cry of grateful love from the crest of joy or the trough of despair; it is a vast, supernatural force that opens out my heart, and binds me close to Jesus."

~St. Thérèse of Lisieux

Pray

God, help me to see that prayer begins with a grateful heart. Open my eyes to my many blessings today.

Act

Write down five things in your life for which you are grateful. Turn one of those grateful thoughts into words or action today. Thankful for your spouse? Tell him so. Grateful for your best friend? Call her or send a note to let her know.

November 2

Think

"The heart is rich when it is content, and it is always content when its desires are fixed on God."

~Bl. Miguel Pro

Pray

Sweet Jesus, remind me moment by moment to thank you. Let me see your hand in my life and let me acknowledge the abundant blessings you shower upon me. Let me see that struggles are blessings too, because they can and do bring me closer to you. Inspire me to tell the world how grateful I am for the gift of life.

Act

Begin a gratitude journal. Each day, record in your own handwriting those things of the day for which you are grateful. Buy a nicely bound book or a spiral sketchbook and some beautiful colored pencils. Take the time to become truly appreciative of God's gifts and aware of your calling in this life. Did you make a list of your hopes back in May? Thank God for his answers.

Think

"When it comes to life the critical thing is whether you take things for granted or take them with gratitude."

~G. K. CHESTERTON

Pray

God, remind me not to take anything for granted. Give to me the gift of sensitivity. Make me ever aware of the many blessings you have bestowed for which I am truly grateful.

Act

People who are survivors—who have survived accidents or illnesses—are often graced with an enhanced appreciation for life. They have learned, through pain and suffering, not to take a moment for granted. That gift is there for each and every one of us. Enjoy your time and your life today. Don't take a moment of it for granted. Take it all with gratitude.

Think

"I would maintain that thanks are the highest form of thought; and that gratitude is happiness doubled by wonder."

~G. K. Chesterton

Pray

God, give me grace to see that I will only be as happy as I make up my mind to be. In every trial today, help me to see a gift, an opportunity, a calling, and a blessing.

Act

Just for today, be obnoxiously grateful. In every thought, in every conversation, find a way to say "thank you." See if it's not contagious.

Think

"Gratitude bestows reverence, allowing us to encounter everyday epiphanies, those transcendent moments of awe that change forever how we experience life and the world."

~John Milton

Pray

Tap me on the shoulder, Lord, and wake me up to your presence and those everyday epiphanies that can be mine if I just tune in to your magnificent plan.

Act

Send someone a thank-you note. Reach way back to someone who taught you something valuable. Did you learn to bake a pie, sail a boat, or create a scrapbook page? Think of some skill you have which you take for granted, and remember the person who gave you that skill. Tell them how much it means to you.

Think

"When we were children we were grateful to those who filled our stockings at Christmas time. Why are we not grateful to God for filling our stockings with legs?"

~G. K. CHESTERTON

Pray

God, help me to see those blessings, especially the small ones, that I fail to recognize in my life. Open my heart and fill it with gratitude for all of your gifts.

Act

Has a priest ever said something in a homily or in confession that helped you grow in faith? Write him a note to thank him for that today. If you can't write him, offer your day for his intentions.

Think

"No gift unrecognized as coming from God is at its own best. . . . When in all gifts we find Him, then in Him we shall find all things."

~George MacDonald

Pray

Dear Lord, please don't let me miss an opportunity to give you all the glory for my gifts. Don't let me be too shy or falsely humble and fail to tell the world that I am nothing without you, but that you have done wondrous things in my life.

Act

Seize the next opportunity to genuinely exclaim out loud, in public, "Thank God!" and mean it.

Think

"Nothing can bring greater happiness than doing God's will for the love of God."

~Bl. Miguel Pro

Pray

Remind me, Lord, that your will for me is not in opposition to my own happiness, but is actually the path to my own happiness. Make me grateful for the crosses you send my way.

Act

Embrace your crosses. Pick something that annoys you—even something small—and give it to God. Attach new meaning to it as an offering of thanksgiving for one of your many blessings.

November 9

Think

"He that complains or murmurs is not perfect, nor is he even a good Christian."

~St. John of the Cross

Pray

As the holiday season approaches, Jesus, make me a humble servant. Infuse me with your spirit of gentle, willing service. Make me truly grateful for the tasks of my vocation. If I begin to complain, silence me. Make me a cheerful giver.

Act

Resist the urge to complain. Ever. Replace complaining words with words of genuine gratitude. Slowly but surely cultivate a habit of gracious gratefulness in your demeanor.

Think

"Oh God, how good you are to allow us to call you 'Our Father.' What gratitude, what joy, what love, and above all what confidence it should inspire in me."

~Ven. Charles de Foucauld

Pray

Father in heaven, I want to love you and lean on you as a child. Thank you for all the ways that you provide for me and take care of me.

Act

Think about what you are good at. Can you write? Sing? Make people laugh? Choose one of your gifts and use it deliberately to bless someone else today. Thank God for your gifts and for the opportunity to share them.

Think

"We should not accept in silence the benefactions of God but return thanks for them."

~St. Basil

Pray

Here I sit before you, God. I will spend the next fifteen minutes listing for you those blessings for which I am truly grateful.

Act

Cut a large tree trunk out of butcher paper and paint it brown. Help your children trace their handprints on autumn-colored construction paper. Cut out the handprints and help them write their blessings on them. Tape or glue them to the trunk to create a Thankful Tree that hangs somewhere prominent in your home.

NOVEMBER 12

Think

"*Give thanks to the Lord, invoke his name; make known among the nations his deeds. Sing to him, sing his praise, proclaim all his wondrous deeds.*"

~1 CHRONICLES 16:8–9

Pray

Lord, I am sorry for the times I have been slow to give thanks and for the blessings I have taken for granted.

Act

Have you ever been hungry—truly hungry? Have you ever had to wonder where your next meal was coming from or how you were going to feed your children? Most of us have not. Sacrifice something today that you normally take for granted (sugar in your tea or butter on your toast), and offer it in thanksgiving for God's abundant blessing.

Think

"Happiness is found only in the home where God is loved and honored, where each one loves, and helps and cares for the others."

~St. Theophane Venard

Pray

Thank you, God, for the gifts of my husband and children. I want every blessing for them. Help me to serve them with a spirit of love and gratitude today.

Act

Does your husband do something routinely that you take for granted, such as taking out the trash or washing your car? Do some small thing for him today without expecting anything in return. Focus on keeping a grateful heart.

Think

"This, then, is the full satisfaction of souls; this is the happy life: to recognize piously and completely the One through whom you are led into the truth, the nature of the truth you enjoy, and the bond that connects you with the supreme measure."

~St. Augustine

Pray

God, I tend to seek satisfaction in everything but you. Draw my attention away from the many "things" I fill my life with and help me to focus more clearly on you—the one who truly satisfies.

Act

Clean out a closet today. Clear out the clutter and set aside clothing and other items to give away. Reflect on God's goodness and, when in doubt, err on the side of generosity.

November 15

Think

"Here ends another day, during which I have had eyes, ears, hands, and the great world around me. Tomorrow begins another day. Why am I allowed two?"

~G. K. Chesterton

Pray

At the end of this day, Lord, make me aware of you in the midst of the people I love. Help me to reflect upon my children and to send them off to sleep with a tenderness that conveys how full my heart is. Let me believe and convey to them that, whatever the cares and burdens, you are in control, and you have plans for our good.

Act

Tonight, when all is quiet, light a candle and pour a glass of wine. Share your gratitude journal with your husband. (Note: Be sure he is listed in those pages before you share!)

Think

"The reason we are not fully at ease in heart and soul is because we seek rest in these things that are so little and have no rest within them, and pay no attention to our God, who is Almighty, All-wise, All-good, and the only real rest."

~BL. JULIAN OF NORWICH

Pray

Whisper in my ear, Lord. Tell me the uncomfortable truth about some earthly attachment that is keeping me from growing closer to you. Help me to remove it from my life.

Act

Is there something you are miserly with? Your time? Your praise? Your money? Your attention? Today, pick that one thing and give it—freely and without counting the cost—to someone who needs it from you most.

Think

"The aim of life is appreciation; there is no sense in not appreciating things; and there is no sense in having more of them if you have less appreciation of them."

~G. K. Chesterton

Pray

Dear God, as I go about my daily duties today, caring for the things in my home, help me to scrutinize the things I touch. Give me a spirit of generosity with my material blessings and a sense of true appreciation for all that I have been given.

Act

It's time for a pre-holiday purge. Gather up as much as you possibly can to donate. If you have two coats, give one away. Push yourself to detach from anything that is cluttering your home and ultimately creating work for you. These are the very things that can bless someone else.

Think

"And Mary said: 'My soul proclaims the greatness of the Lord; my spirit rejoices in God my savior. For he has looked upon his handmaid's lowliness; behold, from now on will all ages call me blessed.'"

~Luke 1:46–48

Pray

Thank you, God, for the gift of Mary, our mother. Help me to grow in love for her and to learn from her example of gratitude and humility.

Act

Mary knew that her gifts and blessings came from God. Have a heart like Mary's today. Before you speak and before you act, ask yourself what Mary would do and say. "Magnify the Lord" in every little thing today.

NOVEMBER 19

Think

"The blessings [God] has given me . . . are the scorn of the world—of its pleasures, its riches, its honor; and the love of the cross, of poverty, of humility; as well as the honor of his constant presence, of familiarity, and intimacy with him; and above all the love of his love."

~BL. MARIE OF THE INCARNATION

Pray

God, it is not gourmet meals and fancy china that I desire. It is humble love around a well-worn table. Help me to create in my kitchen, the heart of my home, a place of comfort for my family and for those who knock at my door. Let me serve with a humble spirit and nourish with a kind heart.

Act

Create a photo collage of your children eating as babies: pictures of nursing infants, babies delighting in their first bites in messy high chairs. Remember the joy of watching them discover the goodness of food and remember that those are the same souls you are feeding today.

November 20

Think

"So abandon yourself utterly for the love of God, and in this way you will become truly happy."

~Bl. Henry Suso

Pray

Jesus, help me to see that you are the path to my happiness. Awaken my senses to feel your love and recognize my reliance on you for every good thing.

Act

Think of something you have complained about recently and turn it around. If there is a chore or circumstance you dislike, give thanks for the opportunity to grow in love. And then . . . get growing!

November 21

Think

"You say grace before meals. All right. But I say grace before the concert and the opera, and grace before the play and pantomime, and grace before I open a book, and grace before sketching, painting, swimming, fencing, boxing, walking, playing, dancing, and grace before I dip the pen in the ink."

~G. K. CHESTERTON

Pray

Everything I do, I am able to do because of you, God. As I begin to cultivate a greater awareness of your abundance, I am increasingly grateful for your blessings. Help me to sanctify each task and joy by whispering a brief prayer of thanks at its beginning.

Act

If you don't say grace as a family before meals, begin this habit today—before each and every meal. If you already say grace before meals, add a grace after meals. If you already say grace before and after meals, choose from G. K. Chesterton's list above and add another "official" moment of gratitude to your day.

Think

"Since I began to love, love has never forsaken me. It has grown to its own fullness within my innermost heart."

~St. Catherine of Genoa

Pray

Open my eyes, Lord. I take so many things for granted that others must do without. Help me to see my many blessings and rejoice in your goodness.

Act

Do you have a little extra of something? Food? Time? Money? Give it away today to someone who needs it. Ask God to show you who can use it most.

Think

"This morning my soul is greater than the world, since it possesses you, you whom heaven and earth do not contain."

~St. Margaret of Cortona (after Holy Communion)

Pray

Jesus, thank you for the gift of yourself in the Eucharist. Make me increasingly aware of the actual grace you give to me each time I receive you. Create in me a greater longing for Holy Communion.

Act

"Eucharist" means thanksgiving. Celebrate Thanksgiving by going to daily Mass as much as you can this week—at the very least, go on Thanksgiving morning.

Think

"Come, let us sing joyfully to the Lord; cry out to the rock of our salvation. Let us greet him with a song of praise, joyfully sing out our psalms."

~PSALM 95:1–2

Pray

God, open my heart and pour in your grace. Let every word I say today and everything I do today be an act of praise and thanksgiving.

Act

Do others know that you are grateful to God for his goodness? In all of your conversations today, look for an opportunity to give credit to God for the ways he has blessed you. Even if you are unaccustomed to speaking openly about your faith, dare to speak words of gratitude and praise to your Father in heaven.

Think

"Never rise from the table, moreover, without having given due thanks to the Lord. If we act in this way we need have no fear of the wretched sin of gluttony. As you eat, take care not to be too difficult to please in the matter of food, bearing in mind that it is very easy to give in to gluttony. Never eat more than you really need."

~St. Padre Pio

Pray

God, you know that this is a week of gluttony in a country of plenty. I beg you for the grace to exercise control over what I eat, to be mindful of your blessings in every bite, and to serve my family good food with a grateful heart. Help me to push away from the table when I have eaten what I need while still celebrating with joy the goodness of your bounty.

Act

As you cook and clean, bake and bustle, don't sin. Remember that the work of your hands is a blessing to your family. Smile while you bless them; rejoice in this opportunity to feed the hungry and give drink to the thirsty. Do it with a genuinely grateful heart.

November 26

Think

"But I am afflicted and in pain; let your saving help protect me, God, that I may praise God's name in song and glorify it with thanksgiving."

~PSALM 69:30–31

Pray

God, help me to remember that words of gratitude are the sweetest prayer I can pray. When I feel too busy to pray, remind me that a whispered "thank you" is often all I need to say.

Act

Think of someone, even someone from your distant past, who has blessed your life in some particular way. Offer a prayer or a small sacrifice in thanksgiving for that person's kindness today.

Think

"When I am, as it were, without feeling, seem unable to pray or practice virtue, that is the time when I must look around for little opportunities, for 'nothings' which please Jesus . . . for example a smile, a kind word."

~St. Thérèse of Lisieux

Pray

Sweet Jesus, remind me that the surest way to "feel," that is to move my emotion toward you, is begin to list those things for which I am grateful. Bring them to my mind and help me to remember how blessed I am and to move through my day ever more aware of how much you love me.

Act

Now that you have gotten into the habit of keeping a gratitude journal, help your children create a gratitude journal too. As we head into a season where they will be bombarded with messages to ask for things, keep focusing them on the many blessings they have already. Set aside just enough time at the end of the day to cultivate this habit together.

November 28

Think

"And as she worshiped the Lord, she said: 'My heart exults in the Lord, my horn is exalted in my God. I have swallowed up my enemies; I rejoice in my victory. There is no Holy One like the Lord; there is no Rock like our God.'"

~1 Samuel 2:1–2

Pray

Lord, give me Hannah's grateful heart today. Give me grace to see all the big ways and small ways I have been undeservedly blessed. Make my heart sing with gratitude.

Act

Make a list. Write the names of your husband and each of your children, and next to each name write three gifts that person has brought into your life. Post the list on the refrigerator or some other place you and your family can see it all day.

Think

"Because I am so weak, you have been pleased to grant my childish little desires, and now you will grant the rest—other desires far greater than the Universe."

~ST. THÉRÈSE OF LISIEUX

Pray

You have given me so much, gracious God. I look over my catalog of blessings this month, and I am moved by your generosity. So often, my prayers are petitions that are tied to this world on earth. Please know that above all, I want most to be with you in heaven.

Act

Take a moment today to thank someone who accepts you despite your weaknesses. These kinds of friends are gifts of the Holy Spirit.

Think

"Enter the temple gates with praise, its courts with thanksgiving. Give thanks to God, bless his name; good indeed is the Lord, whose love endures forever, whose faithfulness lasts through every age."

~Psalm 100:4–5

Pray

Remind me, God, that my ultimate goal is heaven for myself and my family. Faith is a gift none of us deserves. Help me to see your "faithfulness to all generations" in the faces of my children and my parents.

Act

Does a friend or family member not share your gift of faith? Reach out to that person today and offer conversation, an invitation, a small gift, or a note of thanks for their friendship.

DECEMBER

Peace

Think

"For pity's sake, don't start meeting troubles halfway."
~ST. TERESA OF AVILA

Pray

God, remove from my mind all the little worries that threaten my inner peace today. Guide me through the busy days that lie ahead and help me enter this season of Advent with a peaceful heart.

Act

Consider all the work that must be done before Christmas arrives—cooking, shopping, wrapping, and decorating. Decide right now to give it all to God. When you are tempted to panic, place your anxieties at the feet of the pregnant Virgin Mary, full of grace, full of life, and full of joy. Free yourself to embrace all tasks for God's glory.

Think

"Study, my son, to fulfill another man's will rather than your own. Choose always to have little worldly riches rather than much. Seek also the lowest place, and desire to be under others rather than above them; desire and always pray that the will of God be wholly done in you. Lo, such a person enters surely into the very true way of peace and inward quiet."

~THOMAS À KEMPIS

Pray

Dear Lord, help me to remember Thomas à Kempis's "Four Things that Bring Peace to the Soul." Help me notice the needs and desires of the people I love and to fulfill those before I even give thought to my own. I know that you are truly present in poverty and that it is much, much more difficult to see you amidst the plenty of worldly goods.

Act

Make your December to-do list today. If you've already made one, look at it again and reprioritize according to Thomas à Kempis's advice and the prayer above.

December 3

Think

"You must never be discouraged or give way to anxiety . . .
but ever have recourse to the adorable Heart of Jesus."

~St. Margaret Mary Alacoque

Pray

I know, Lord, that you are all I ever need, but I need
you to show me that today. Enter into my heart and
soul. Give me the peace that can only come from you.

Act

Whatever small tasks you must perform today, focus
on them and them alone. Are you folding laundry?
Baking cookies? Planning dinner? Kissing boo-boos?
It is enough.

December 4

Think

"The real problem of the Christian life comes where people do not usually look for it. It comes the very moment you wake up each morning. All your wishes and hopes for the day rush at you like wild animals. And the first job each morning consists simply in shoving them all back; in listening to that other voice, taking that other point of view, letting that other larger, stronger, quieter life come flowing in. And so on, all day. Standing back from all your natural fussings and frettings; coming in out of the wind."

~C. S. Lewis

Pray

God of Peace, give me the grace to shove away the fussings and frettings of the season in order to make room for the quieter life you offer to me.

Act

Come in out of the wind today. No matter where you live, take time this afternoon to sit down with your children, drink hot chocolate stirred with a candy cane and read a story appropriate for the season.

Think

"Learn to let others do their share of the work. Things may be done less well, but you will have more peace of soul and health of body. And what temporal interest should we not sacrifice in order to gain these blessings?"

~ST. PHILIPPINE DUCHESNE

Pray

God, I know that we will never know true perfection until we meet you in heaven. Give me grace to accept imperfection. Help me to let go of the things that do not matter and hold fast to you.

Act

If you buy or make a small gift today, plan for one extra. Use it to surprise an acquaintance or even a stranger during this season of preparation. Choose someone you normally would not buy a present for—a grocery store clerk, your hairdresser, or someone you see at church.

December 6

Think

"The giver of every good and perfect gift has called upon us to mimic His giving, by grace, through faith, and this is not of ourselves."

~St. Nicholas

Pray

Jesus, the gifts I give that have the most enduring value are gifts of time and service. Through the intercession of St. Nicholas on his special feast day, I beg you to give me the grace and strength to be very, very generous this Advent with those gifts of great worth.

Act

Offer to do some shopping for a friend or neighbor who might not be able to get out and about. In this day of internet accessibility, it need not be a local friend. Far away elderly friends may not have your computer savvy and might be grateful for your gift of time and service.

DECEMBER 7

Think

"Do not lose your inward peace for anything whatsoever, even if your whole world seems upset."

~ST. FRANCIS DE SALES

Pray

God, help me to see how worry robs me of joy. Help me to conquer my fears by placing my trust in you.

Act

Is there someone you have offended? Even if you "know" you are right and they are wrong, call that person today, say you are sorry, and make amends.

December 8

Think

"Humility does not disturb or disquiet, however great it may be; it comes with peace, delight, and calm. . . . Pain of genuine humility doesn't agitate or afflict the soul; rather, this humility expands it and enables it to serve God alone."

~St. Teresa of Avila

Pray

God, please quiet the cacophony of voices that call to women at this time of year. I am preparing for a Holy Infant, not running a marathon of entertaining and excess. Quiet my spirit and remind me to help my family prepare for the Baby, just as Mary quietly trod toward Bethlehem.

Act

Today, on the Feast of the Immaculate Conception, meditate on the spotless soul of the Blessed Mother. How much room is there for God's infinite grace! If confession is available before Mass today, go! Make room in your soul for all the graces you will need for this season.

DECEMBER 9

Think

"By the anxieties and worries of this life Satan tries to dull man's heart and make a dwelling for himself there."

~St. Francis of Assisi

Pray

Give me a simple heart, Lord. Remove from it all distraction and fill it instead with your love and your peace. Help me to see others as you see them and love them as you do.

Act

Make a secret surprise for someone in your family today. Do one of your husband's chores and keep quiet about it. Leave a love note in someone's bag or on their pillow.

December 10

Think

"First, have peace in thy own breast, then thou wilt be qualified to restore peace to others. Peacefulness is a more useful acquisition than learning."

~Thomas à Kempis

Pray

Jesus, you have such a heart for the littlest child. Help me to remember today that the frenzy preceding Christmas can be stressful for a small child. Open my heart to your grace and your peace so that I can bring that peace to my children.

Act

Take your time with the bedtime wind-down tonight. Before you even begin, pray for your own peace of heart. Then, take time with baths and bedtime stories and prayers and pillow talk. If your children are all older, share a cup of something hot and give them your undivided attention before bedtime. Bring peace into their dreams—and yours.

December 11

Think

"Wisdom enters through love, silence, and mortification. It is great wisdom to know how to be silent and to look at neither the remarks, nor the deeds, nor the lives of others."

~St. John of the Cross

Pray

God, when I am tempted to judge others or compare myself to them, help me to focus instead on my own faults and my own work toward holiness. Open my eyes to the ways in which you are calling me closer to you today.

Act

Is there someone in your life you are tempted to envy? Thank God for the generous gifts he has given that person. Make some small sacrifice today and offer it for that person's intentions.

Think

"Am I not here, I, who am your Mother? Are you not under my shadow and protection? Am I not the source of your joy? Are you not in the hollow of my mantle, in the crossing of my arms? Do you need anything more? Let nothing else worry you, disturb you."

~OUR LADY OF GUADALUPE TO ST. JUAN DIEGO

Pray

Through the intercession of Our Lady of Guadalupe, I beg you, Lord, to make me as faithful as Juan Diego. Let nothing worry me. Let nothing disturb me. Instead, let me feel the warmth and security of the Blessed Mother's mantle.

Act

Make a Mexican feast tonight in honor of the Feast of Our Lady of Guadalupe and St. Juan Diego. In a pinch, Mexican takeout will do. Remember, it's a feast day! Take a deep breath, let go of the Christmas preparation crazies, and just enjoy your family.

Think

"While you are proclaiming peace with your lips, be careful to have it even more fully in your heart."

~St. Francis of Assisi

Pray

Lord, help me to practice what I preach. Make me an example of quiet, gentle love for my children today. Even when I am angry or upset, give me peace to speak calmly and with great love.

Act

Skip all unnecessary activities this afternoon and do something fun with your kids. Say "yes" to some taxing but kid-friendly activity you tend to avoid—finger paints, crafting, baking cookies, or playing outdoors.

December 14

Think

"The faith of those who live their faith is a serene faith. What you long for will be given you; what you love will be yours forever. Since it is by giving alms that everything is pure for you, you will also receive that blessing which is promised next by the Lord: the Godhead that no man has been able to see. In the inexpressible joy of this eternal vision, human nature will possess what eye has not seen or ear heard, what man's heart has never conceived."

~St. Leo the Great

Pray

God of light, show me where you would have me give today. Grant me the peace that passes understanding.

Act

With your children, give today. Whether you shop for an Angel Tree gift, seek out the Salvation Army, bring Christmas flowers to a nursing home, help an elderly neighbor decorate, or deliver cookies to someone who would have none . . . give!

Think

"In everything, whether it is a thing sensed or a thing known, God himself is hidden within."

~St. Bonaventure

Pray

Help me to see you in all my little moments today, God. Open my eyes to the peace and the beauty that are all around but that I am usually too busy to see.

Act

Take a walk today with someone you love. Breathe the fresh air, enjoy the change of scenery, and listen—*really listen*—to whatever your loved one wants to share with you.

DECEMBER 16

Think

"Do not be disturbed by the clamor of the world that passes like a shadow."

~St. Clare of Assisi

Pray

Infant Lord, the world becomes noisier and noisier as we approach your birthday. Help me to remember that infants are best appreciated in the quiet.

Act

Reserve a half hour of quiet for yourself today. Fix a cup of something warm, and curl up with the Bible or an Advent book. Read, or don't—the important thing is the quiet. Listen. Jesus is speaking.

December 17

Think

"True humility doesn't come to the soul with agitation or disturbance, nor does it darken it or bring dryness. Rather, true humility consoles and acts in a completely opposite way: quietly, gently, and with light."

~St. Teresa of Avila

Pray

Lord, help me to stop asserting my own will against yours. Help me to forget myself and open my heart to wherever you are leading me today. Quiet my soul so I can hear your voice.

Act

When you are tempted to turn on TV for the kids today, don't. Instead, invite them to sit with you and read stories. Tell the story of Joseph and Mary making their way to Bethlehem, and thank God for the blessings he has given your family this Advent.

DECEMBER 18

Think

"First keep the peace within yourself, then you can also bring peace to others."

~THOMAS À KEMPIS

Pray

They need me, God. All these people in my home are busy and tired and approaching a frenzy of excitement. Let me achieve a peace of heart that I can transmit to them. Help me bring your peace to this season of joyful anticipation.

Act

Remember that you are not Martha Stewart, nor do you aspire to be her. You aspire to be more like Mary than Martha. Take some time today to set aside the lists and inspirations of merry-making. Instead, read of Mary and Joseph's journey to Bethlehem. Talk to Mary early and often today! The people around you most need a collected woman striving to live in holiness.

December 19

Think

"It is our part to offer what we can, his to finish what we cannot."

~St. Jerome

Pray

God, I am sometimes tempted to rely on my own strength to get me through trying times. Today, help me to see that without you I can do nothing. Help me to keep you at the center of all that I do.

Act

Bring the kids with you to a grocery store. Purchase as many food items as you can afford to donate and drop them off at a food pantry on the way home. Make a simple dinner for your own family and thank God for the food he provides.

DECEMBER 20

Think

"Why should we defend ourselves when we are misunderstood and misjudged? Let us leave that aside. Let us not say anything. It is so sweet to let others judge us in any way they like. O blessed silence, which gives so much peace to the soul!"

~St. Thérèse of Lisieux

Pray

St. Thérèse, you understood well what it was to work hard in a thousand little ways and still be unappreciated. Help me to keep giving and to stop worrying about how my efforts are judged. Don't let me waste time explaining myself. Ask God to turn my attention, instead, to him and to remember that everything I do, I do for the glory of God.

Act

Do something today for someone who is predictably critical of you. Offer it sincerely and joyfully, and don't think twice about how it will be received.

DECEMBER 21

Think

"Once you have realized you are in the presence of God, cast yourself down with deep reverence before him and acknowledge your unworthiness to appear in his majestic presence, asking for all the graces you need to serve him well, knowing that in his goodness he longs to grant them to you."

~ST. FRANCIS DE SALES

Pray

Shower me with your grace today, O Lord. Fill me up where I am lacking. Give me faith. Give me hope. Give me peace.

Act

Arrange to visit someone or phone someone you know is alone. See Christ in that person and be Christ to that person.

Think

"He did not say: 'You will not be assailed, you will not be belabored, you will not be disquieted,' but he said: 'You will not be overcome.'"

~BL. JULIAN OF NORWICH

Pray

Dear God, I am so tired, and yet there are so many little details to which I must attend. Help me to remember all day today that, as long as I work toward loving you well, I will not be overcome.

Act

Take time tonight to sit with your husband and reminisce about Christmases past. Dwell only on the very happy shared memories. Our joys are abundant, despite the effort raising a family entails.

DECEMBER 23

Think

"When the angels went away from them to heaven, the shepherds said to one another, 'Let us go, then, to Bethlehem to see this thing that has taken place, which the Lord has made known to us.'"

~LUKE 2:15

Pray

In all my busyness today, God, turn my heart toward you. I am tired and distracted, but I never want to forget that we are preparing to receive you. Prepare my heart to receive the gift of God this Christmas.

Act

Are you holding onto a grudge or some hurtful event from your past? Give it to God today. Say a prayer for the person who wronged you or better yet, call that person and make peace.

Think

"Never be hurried by anything whatever—nothing can be more pressing than the necessity for your peace before God. You will help others more by the peace and tranquility of your heart than by any eagerness or care you can bestow on them."

~St. Elizabeth Ann Seton

Pray

St. Elizabeth Ann Seton, you knew well what it was like to prepare to celebrate Christmas in a house full of children. Please pray that I will be reminded all day long today, despite my most pressing duties, that it is the peace of Christ we will welcome tonight. Pray that the baby might bring tranquility to my heart and that I may bring his holy peace to everyone I meet tonight and tomorrow.

Act

Take a few minutes sometime today or tonight to be still in front of the crèche. Open your heart to the peace of Christ and just sit, admiring the baby.

December 25

Think

"For a child is born to us, a son is given us; upon his shoulder dominion rests. They name him Wonder-Counselor, God-Hero, Father-Forever, Prince of Peace."

~Isaiah 9:5

Pray

Come into my heart today, Baby Jesus. Come into my home. May your peace and love reign here forever.

Act

Whatever your plans for celebrating this special day, take some time to sit in a quiet place and thank Jesus for the gift of his coming.

December 26

Think

"O tender Father, You gave me more, much more, than I ever thought to ask for. Thank you, and again thank you, O Father, for having granted my requests, and for having granted those things that I never realized I needed or sought."

~St. Catherine of Siena

Pray

It is the day after the great feast, dear Lord. And I feel the inevitable deflation in my household. Help me to remind my children that your gifts are more precious than anything they unwrapped yesterday. Help me to live Christmas throughout this holy season and bring your peace into our new year.

Act

Help your children write thank-you notes today. Provide paper, fun pens, stickers, and plenty of assistance as necessary.

DECEMBER 27

Think

"Be at peace with your own soul, then heaven and earth will be at peace with you."

~St. Jerome

Pray

Lord, thank you for the gifts of my talents and abilities. Help me to see my circumstances, my skills, and my personality as part of your plan for my life and use these gifts to serve you always.

Act

What is something you are especially good at? Cooking? Organizing? Listening? Making friendly conversation? Think of someone who could benefit from that gift and share it with them today.

DECEMBER 28

Think

"Celebrate the feast of Christmas every day, even every moment in the interior temple of your spirit, remaining like a baby in the bosom of the heavenly Father, where you will be reborn each moment in the Divine Word, Jesus Christ."

~St. Paul of the Cross

Pray

Christmas is a season, Lord, but the peace of Christ in the stable can live within me all year round. As I meditate upon the baby wrapped in the mantle of the Blessed Mother, give me the grace to remember that his birth puts me there, too. Let me be reborn again every day in the Word.

Act

Take a look around your home. Is it more obvious during Christmastime that a Christian family lives there? Make a list of plans for bringing reminders of Christ into your environment all year long. Perhaps spend Christmas money on a statue or an icon.

DECEMBER 29

Think

"Everybody today seems to be in such a terrible rush; anxious for greater developments and greater wishes and so on; so that children have very little time for their parents; Parents have very little time for each other; and the home begins the disruption of the peace of the world."

~Bl. Teresa of Calcutta

Pray

Help me to slow down, Lord. When my work feels like too much, remind me that I can do all things through you. Remind me to rely on you instead of counting on my own efforts.

Act

Don't hurry today. Take time to watch snow fall or birds fly, join a toddler in an imaginary game, teach an older child to sew, knit, or cook. Don't rush—pay attention to little details and find beauty in those.

Think

"Who except God can give you peace? Has the world ever been able to satisfy the heart?"

~St. Gerard Majella

Pray

Remind me, Lord, of all the times I've looked to the world to satisfy the longing in my heart. Teach me again the lessons of those disappointments. As I make resolutions, grant me the strength of will to turn away from the incessant call of the world and rest in you alone.

Act

Take advantage of the relative quiet of post-Christmas days in the secular world to extend genuine hospitality. Reconnect with old friends over a potluck dinner or dessert.

Think

"In contrast, the fruit of the Spirit is love, joy, peace, patience, kindness, generosity, faithfulness, gentleness, self-control. Against such there is no law."

~GALATIANS 5:22–23

Pray

Thank you, God, for the year that has passed. Thank you for the blessings and the challenges, and all the little ways you have called me closer to you. In the coming year give me grace to serve my family well and to know and do your will in all the joys and sorrows that lie ahead.

Act

Even if you don't plan to stay up until midnight, make plans for a special celebration with your family tonight. Break open a bottle of champagne or sparkling cider, and take turns thanking God for the blessings of the past year.

Danielle Bean is editor-in-chief of *Catholic Digest*, which has a readership of more than 1.5 million. She is also the host of *The Gist*, a television talk show for Catholic women on the CatholicTV network. Bean is author of *My Cup of Tea: Musings of a Catholic Mom* and *Mom to Mom, Day to Day: Advice and Support for Catholic Living*. She is a popular speaker on a variety of subjects related to Catholic family life, homeschooling, marriage, and motherhood. Bean lives in New Hampshire with her husband and their eight children.

Elizabeth Foss is a cancer survivor who lives every day grateful for the gift of life. Married to Mike Foss and mother to nine children, she finds the charm, wonder, and cacophony of big family imperfection to be great inspiration as she strives to meet life with creativity and grace. A graduate of the University of Virginia, Foss has written an award-winning family life column for the *Arlington Catholic Herald* since 1993. Her writing appears frequently in *Catholic Digest* and has been published by *Catholic Exchange*, EWTN, and the *Washington Post*. She is the author of *Real Learning* and lives in Virginia.